A Guide to Print, Photograph, Architecture & Ephemera Collections

at The New-York Historical Society

by
Helena Zinkham

Published by
The New-York Historical Society
New York City
1998

For Cole, Elizabeth, and Natalie;
for the future to know the past.

Text and design © 1998 by Helena Zinkham
Book design by Diane Tod South
All drawings, prints, and photographs courtesy of The New-York Historical Society.
All rights reserved.

Figure 1. *Mrs. Frederick Charles Jennings and Miss Annie Louise M. Jennings (later Mrs. Howard Masten Canoune) on front porch of Dellbrook, the Jennings residence in Plainfield, N.J.* Photograph by Howard Masten Canoune, August 1908. (Album File, neg. no. 59249)

The Historical Society preserves photographs that can evoke the past for many people while portraying one family's memories. Real estate lawyer Howard Canoune (1871–1934) compiled several albums to document his family's life from the 1890s to 1920s. Canoune married Annie Jennings a few months after making this graceful portrait of a mother and daughter reading a letter.

Figure 2. Baseball game at the old Polo Grounds, Fifth Avenue and 110th Street, New York City. Copy of photograph by Richard Hoe Lawrence, May 31, 1886. (Lawrence Collection, neg. no. 32485)

One city's local history often represents American history. Baseball's popularity as a national pastime is evident in the crowded stands and large advertising signs that form the backdrop for this early sports action photograph. The National League New York Giants are playing on their home field in Manhattan against the Boston Beaneaters.

Contents

Preface
7

Acknowledgments
8

Introduction
11

Bibliography
38

The Collections
43

Chronological Index
159

General Index
167

Figure 3. Times Square on a rainy night, New York City. View looking north along Broadway and Seventh Avenue from about 45th Street. Gelatin silver print by Browning, 1923. (Browning Collection, neg. no. 58362)

Photographs related to New York City predominate in the Society's pictorial collections. Images such as this view of the north end of Times Square (later called Duffy Square) convey the energy of the Big Apple. The commercial photographer's eye illustrates how Broadway, with its huge lighted advertising signs and numerous movie theaters, deserved to be called the Great White Way. Little caption information came with this collection. For example, this photograph's date was devised by checking when the movies named on the marquees were released. Both the *Hunchback of Notre Dame* and *Rosita* opened in 1923.

Preface

It is my great pleasure to welcome you to this guide to the print, photograph, architecture, and ephemera collections of The New-York Historical Society. For the first time, researchers will be able to learn about these materials through a single catalog that describes the 75 separate collections that house some 1 million items in all.

In the nearly 200 years since its founding in 1804, the Historical Society has collected a vast range of visual materials that illuminate American history. These collections have proved invaluable to historians, documentary filmmakers, architects, novelists, artists, teachers, and many others interested in visual records of the past. Through this guide, these resources now will be available to an even wider audience.

The scope of the collections described in this guide includes not only New York's past but the nation's. In addition to unparalleled views of the city, researchers can find unique materials documenting the American Revolution, the Civil War, the gold rush, and many other important moments in our history. There is also much that illustrates everyday life in the American past through photo albums, posters, and advertisements.

Helena Zinkham deserves great praise for her fascinating overview of the Historical Society's holdings and her concise summaries of each collection. Researchers will find it hard to resist taking a look into the collections she so temptingly describes.

Finally, we salute our generous sponsors, who together have made this invaluable resource possible: The Bay Foundation, whose confidence at a challenging time led the way; and the John Watts de Peyster endowment fund, allowing Society publications that promote the study of American history. The Society also salutes the New York State Education Department, whose annual library operating support makes the collections described here available to the visiting public. And we gratefully acknowledge public funds from the New York City Department of Cultural Affairs, which provide generous support for library services.

Betsy Gotbaum, Executive Director
The New-York Historical Society

Acknowledgments

When the Society decided to increase access to its Print Room collections in 1980, Director James J. Heslin and Librarian Larry Sullivan hired me to prepare a catalog and expand reference services. Although officially one of the Society's two curators of prints, I worked chiefly as a librarian and archivist to compile an in-house guide to the photograph, architecture, ephemera, and print collections in the Print Room's care. We wanted to publish a more comprehensive guide, but in 1984 I moved to Washington, D.C., to work at the Library of Congress, Prints and Photographs Division. In order to complete the project, I enjoyed many return visits to New York and continued to work with Print Room staff to sort, identify, index, and study key materials. Superb historical reference resources at the Library of Congress provided valuable background information for many collections. The Society's Director of Development Paul Gunther successfully raised the funds needed to publish this book in the 1990s.

The *Guide* would not have been possible, of course, without the valuable contributions of many Print Room staff members. I am especially indebted to Curator of Photographs Dale Neighbors, who processed several large collections and reviewed each entry, while bringing much new material to light through exhibitions and improving storage conditions. Esther Brumberg single-handedly added records for several thousand items to the Negative File catalog and cleared one large storage room by integrating its contents into the appropriate collections. Decorative arts specialist Nina Gray made considerable progress with the architecture collections, reclaimed thousands of glass negatives from remote storage, and uncovered many striking images in partially cataloged files. Curator of Prints Wendy Shadwell and Curator of Architecture Mary Beth Betts commented on each entry in their respective specialty areas. Staff members Nancy Bender, Diana Kane, Laird Ogden, Pat Paladines, Catherine Schmidt, and Darlene Scriven counted, re-housed, and labeled tens of thousands of items. Their efforts refined impressions of collections that have been available for years and brought many new images into use.

For inspiration and advice along the way, I am grateful to Judy Cooke, Lynn Cox, and Elisabeth Parker, who taught me well about libraries and special collections. Georgia Barnhill (American Antiquarian Society), Andrew Eskind (George Eastman House), Christopher Gray (Office for Metropolitan History), Mary Ison (Library of Congress), Janet Parks (Avery Architectural and Fine Arts Library), and Larry Sullivan (John Jay College) read the manuscript and provided valuable encouragement and suggestions. Diane South (Agave Communications) designed the layout integrating text and illustrations. Her persistence and friendship often kept this project afloat. I am also grateful to my husband and parents for their long support while I pored over old papers and pictures.

Helena Zinkham
Arlington, Virginia

Figure 4. Hester Street, west from and including the southwest corner of Norfolk Street, New York City. Photograph by unidentified photographer, ca. 1898.
(Geographic File, neg. no. 37363)

Many Jewish, Italian, and other immigrants who arrived in the United States in the late 1880s lived in overcrowded conditions on Manhattan's Lower East Side, including Hester Street, which appears here with many pushcart vendors. This photograph demonstrates the Society's long commitment to documenting New York City's rapidly changing physical appearance. The image was accessioned in 1912, and staff researched the picture by noting such details as the vacant fenced area, where slum tenements were demolished to create Seward Park, and the multistory frame houses (on the right) that were later cut down to one-story stores.

Introduction

People engaged in many pursuits depend on pictorial materials to illuminate the past. Biographers and historians understand their subjects better by viewing portraits and street scenes from various time periods. Historic preservationists use architectural drawings and photographs when planning building restorations. Documentary film makers and book publishers search for illustrations to bring their stories to life. Curators select striking material to exhibit. Teachers identify images to train students to interpret history and to develop critical thinking skills and visual literacy. Whether to satisfy personal curiosity or to gain scholarly insight, many people can benefit from repositories of visual history (Figure 1). This *Guide to Print, Photograph, Architecture & Ephemera Collections at The New-York Historical Society* is designed to improve access to the Society' extraordinary and extensive pictorial resources. The *Guide* is the first general catalog for the Department of Prints, Photographs, and Architecture—an orientation to an estimated 1 million items in 75 separate collections and files.

While people who need visual information about New York City often turn naturally to The New-York Historical Society because of its name, the Society's Department of Prints, Photographs, and Architecture also has many images related to pre-1900 United States history and culture in general (Figure 2). Major subject strengths include portraits of national leaders, theatrical celebrities, and New York society figures through 1920; views of major United States cities through 1860; bird's-eye panoramas of New York state communities through 1900; New York City views through 1940 (Figures 3 and 4), especially Manhattan architecture, elevated railroads, subways, and fires; and images documenting naval history and maritime transportation. Also plentiful are political cartoons from the Revolutionary War through Theodore Roosevelt's presidency, California gold rush material, Civil War prints and photographs, business and advertising ephemera, and posters. The early American engravings, lithographs, architectural drawings, daguerreotypes, stereographs, photomechanical prints, and tradecards provide much raw material for art historians and students of popular culture to study the development of graphic arts and photography in the United States.

This *Guide* will assist both novice and experienced researchers. Those who already have a question to pursue can consult the *Guide* indexes to select pertinent collections to explore. Browsing through the *Guide* also will provide an overview of the collections and suggest new topics to investigate.[1] For example, more than 50 well-known and forgotten architects, photographers, and printmakers are represented by enough material to support in-depth studies of their lives and works, among them architect George B. Post, professional photographer Burr McIntosh, amateur photographer Robert L. Bracklow, and poster producers at the Strobridge Lithographing Company. The examination of several collections together could aid understanding of the history of photography: Clarence White's role in pictorialism (Antoinette B. Hervey and Doris Ulmann studied with him); Society of Amateur Photographers' activities (Robert L. Bracklow and Richard H. Lawrence won exhibition prizes during Alfred Stieglitz's early years at the club); careers of professional women photographers (Jessie Tarbox Beals and Mattie Edwards Hewitt) and of photographers who specialized in portraits of men (Theron Kilmer and Pirie MacDonald).

Research with pictorial materials is often as complex as it is rewarding. Pictorial research can be simplified by answering the following questions before beginning a project:

1. How exhaustive a search do you plan to make, and how much time do you have to spend?
2. What institutions will you consult to do the research?
3. Do you need to see original materials, or will reproductions suffice?
4. What kinds of copies will you want? Xerographic or photographic, color or black-and-white?
5. What types of pictorial material do you want to see? Is the medium or format important? Should the images be contemporary to the historical event or can they be an artist's interpretation? (Figures 5 and 6)
6. Do you have enough information about the topic to supply dates or names of individuals, locations, and events associated with it?
7. Do you have enough information about the topic to be able to evaluate and interpret the images you find? Do you need to read about visual literacy skills first?[2]

---

[1] Requests for copies of Society images seen in publications are best answered by contacting the Society's Department of Rights and Reproductions, 170 Central Park West, New York, New York 10024-5194.

[2] John and Barbara Schultz provide additional guidance in *Picture Research: A Practical Guide* (New York: Van Nostrand Reinhold, 1991). Thomas Schlereth outlines evaluation criteria for photographs that are primary research information sources in "Mirror Images," in *Artifacts and the American Past* (Nashville: American Association for State and Local History, 1980), 11-47.

Figure 5. *The Newsboys' Picnic— Tumbling into the Water.* Wood engraving from a drawing by C.S. Reinhart. Published in *Harper's Weekly,* August 30, 1873, p. 757. (Peters Collection, neg. no. 64183)

Figure 6. *Coney Island.* Platinum photograph by Robert L. Bracklow, 1902. (Bracklow Collection, neg. no. 60884)

Knowing what types of images are available for different time periods simplifies picture research. For action scenes of the 1800s, consult collections of engravings or lithographs based on artists' drawings. The first practical photographic processes appeared in 1839, and photographic views with people in motion were rare until the 1890s. These two images of people at beaches illustrate the different impressions created by the print and photographic formats.

Figures **7** and **8**. George Washington Bridge, between Fort Lee, New Jersey, and West 178th Street, New York City. Photographs by Ernest L. Scott. Left: *Both towers and north anchor from hillside between Riverside Drive and Haven Avenue,* 1929. (Geographic File, neg. no. 61772) Right: *Looking down the south cables toward New York,* 1931. (Geographic File, neg. no. 61741)

It often takes more than one picture to tell a compelling story. These two views, from a series by amateur photographer Ernest Scott, document interesting features of the massive George Washington Bridge construction project, which lasted from 1926 to 1931. The photograph on the left, taken from the Manhattan shore looking across the Hudson River toward New Jersey, shows the towers, anchors, and cables that preceded the roadway. The photograph of the completed bridge illustrates the impressive technology of suspension bridges. If you look carefully, you'll see an airship in the sky and the Little Red Lighthouse at the base of the tower.

A sample search for images related to the George Washington Bridge illustrates the steps involved. Reference books supply the information that O.H. Ammann and Cass Gilbert designed this impressive suspension bridge, which opened in 1931 and spans the Hudson River between upper Manhattan and New Jersey. The *Guide*'s index has one entry under the bridge's name. It points to a group of photographs taken during construction by a local enthusiast, Ernest L. Scott. Additional material is found by looking up the names of the bridge designers. While nothing is listed under Ammann, a large body of material is available under Cass Gilbert. By generalizing the topic to the

Hudson River or Manhattan and by limiting it through the *Guide*'s chronological index to the 1920s or later, other files are found that might be worth consulting. The Browning Photograph Collection, Geographic File, McLaughlin Air Service Photograph Collection, and Postcard File all match the general subject and time period. Were there elevated railroads or subway stations near the bridge's Manhattan terminus? Under those subjects, the *Guide*'s index lists two entries that might have pertinent images: the Green and Subway transportation photograph collections. Would images of boats passing under the bridge offer interesting views of the bridge? Under ships and steamboats, the index mentions the Murdock and Scanlon collections. Was the bridge featured in any advertising campaigns or civic celebrations? The index entries under advertisements refer to the Landauer Collection and the Poster File, which could have colorful ephemera about the bridge.

After drawing up a list of likely collections from the *Guide* indexes and entries, the next step is to write or visit the Society to consult the finding aids for individual collections for more specific information. Continuing with the example, the Gilbert Collection indexes indicate that preliminary sketches and working drawings as well as correspondence files exist for the bridge. By examining this archive, it is possible to obtain the political as well as the design history of the bridge and trace its progress as it was scaled back from stone-clad arches to the skeletal steel structure visible today. The Browning Collection inventory has no entries under bridges, and the collection can be skipped. The Geographic File finding aid lists folders for bridges. Upon checking the folders, the researcher will find several clear overviews by commercial photographers. Photographs by Ernest Scott will provide detailed views of the towers, trusses, roadways, and opening parade (Figures 7 and 8). The McLaughlin Collection will contribute informative aerial photographs that clarify the bridge's role in connecting New York City and New Jersey. The Negative File catalog also should be consulted, as with any query, because it provides a centralized index to original and copy negatives of material in many collections throughout the Society. Entries under "New York City—Bridges" lead, for example, to a colorful souvenir kerchief.

The search could extend to the Society's Library Reading Room, Manuscript Department, and Department of Paintings, Sculpture, and Decorative Arts, which might also have pertinent material. Other institutions strong in New York City history or civil engineering might also be consulted: the Museum of the City of New York, the New York Public Library, the New York City Archives, the Library of Congress, the Avery Architectural and Fine Arts Library at Columbia University, and the National Museum of American History. The following history of the Society's pictorial collections further explains their strengths and the complementary relationships to collections in other departments.

History and scope of the collections

The New-York Historical Society is one of the oldest independent research libraries and museums in the United States. In 1804, city clerk John Pintard led a group of prominent New Yorkers to found the Society with the ambitious mission "to discover, procure, and preserve whatever may relate to the natural, civil, literary, and ecclesiastical history of the United States in general, and of this State in particular." (Figure 9) Many of the early members were active in the political, economic, and cultural development of the new nation. Egbert Benson, the Society's first president, was a Revolutionary patriot, congressman, and judge. DeWitt Clinton, the third president, served

Figure 9. Armorial bookplate for John Pintard. Engraving by Alexander Anderson, 1800 or later. (Bookplate File, neg. no. 64239)

John Pintard (1759–1844) led the men who founded The New-York Historical Society in 1804. His bookplate motto, "Never Despair," aptly reflects the perseverance required from both Pintard and other members to keep the Society going. The collections grew steadily, but financial difficulties left the Society's future uncertain. It shared six temporary quarters with other organizations until it opened its own library and gallery on Second Avenue in 1857.

several terms as New York City mayor and state governor and also sponsored the construction of the Erie Canal. Several leading artists and authors, among them Alexander Anderson, Asher B. Durand, John Trumbull, Washington Irving, and George Bancroft, were members who contributed to both the collections and lecture programs.

During the Society's first century, its gentlemen scholars sought out chiefly books and manuscripts to document the nation's history. The importance of visual materials was acknowledged, though, in the listing of almost 50 engraved views and portraits in the Society's first catalog, published in 1813. As the Society grew, it assembled an outstanding library of books, maps, and documents and filled its public galleries with valuable paintings and sculpture. Strong statements about the importance of visual documentation appeared in the 1862 *Annual Report of the Committee on the Fine Arts,* including enthusiastic support for the then relatively new medium of photography.

> …An important part of the labor of historians has been to describe past scenes and personages… Often, indeed, as Rembrandt, with a few old turbans and shawls, made up a gorgeous oriental tableau, so they have been forced to construct the most splendid dramatic picture out of the slenderest supply of properties and costumes. If Art had been able to preserve for them the actual reflections, as in a looking-glass, of the scenes they describe, what life would animate, what truth would dignify their pages!… How many questions it would solve in architecture, and costume, and history, about which hundreds of dull and unsatisfactory books have been written!
>
> As it is one of the chief objects of our Society to accumulate materials for the use of future historical students, it is most evident that we should carefully provide for the collection of photographs—not only the likenesses of eminent men and women, but views of streets, houses, landscapes, processions, reviews, battles, and sieges, and indeed almost everything which can be photographed. These should be carefully marked, dated, indexed, classified, and pasted in books. They seem to be small and unimportant by themselves, but when arranged in this way in large numbers, and with proper conveniences of reference, they would undoubtedly form the most valuable auxiliaries to historical inquiry that we could hand down to our successors.

Acquisition of pictorial materials focused on portraits and views through the rest of the 1800s, with some donations of architectural drawings and ephemera.

The Society's move to larger quarters in 1908 brought the graphic collections into greater prominence through exhibitions that chronicled New York City and the maritime life that shaped its history. Through the 1930s, interest in early American history remained strong. In 1918, the Society's Field Exploration Committee began to document Revolutionary War camp sites, and in 1920 Dr. George W. Nash donated his negatives of East Coast buildings and artifacts. Descendants of John McComb presented his architectural drawings for New York City Hall, completed in 1812.

Society president Samuel V. Hoffman donated many prize photographs, including a set of rare calotypes by Victor Prevost, which are among the earliest photographic views of New York City. The Society also responded to current events in world history by acquiring hundreds of World War I posters. During the 1920s, Bella C. Landauer started her extraordinary business and advertising ephemera collection. Harold Seton and Gertrude and Raphael Weed presented their extensive portrait collections of New York actors. Staff reported that card catalogs of prints, engraved portraits, photographs, lithographs, negatives, and lantern slides were complete. The Society amended its charter to acknowledge its commitment to education, and among other activities offered free sets of almost 100 historical illustrations to schools. In 1931, an in-house photographic lab was installed.

When new wings were added to the Society's headquarters in 1938, a separate library department, called the Map and Print Room, was established for the graphic collections (Figure 10). In 1942, M. Bartlett Cowdrey became the first curator in charge of maps, atlases, broadsides, prints, photographs, and drawings. Her successor, Arthur B. Carlson, oversaw the department's growth from 1943 to 1965. The staff, which varied from two to three people, soon reported that a new catalog for New York City views was almost complete. They also implemented a general classification scheme to arrange the collections. Generous donors of prints in the 1930s and 1940s included Henry O. Havemeyer, Harry T. Peters, and James Boyd. During the 1940s and 1950s, Society Direc-

Figure 10. *The New-York Historical Society.* Etching by Ernest D. Roth, 1939 or 1940. (The New-York Historical Society Pictorial Archive, neg. no. 31305)

In 1903–08, the Society built its current headquarters (its eighth home) on Central Park West. Thirty years later, the Society expanded again by adding two wings to fill the block between 76th and 77th Streets. In 1938, the Society also established a Map and Print Room to provide more attention for the graphic collections. The Department's scope gradually changed to focus on pictorial collections, and its current name is the Department of Prints, Photographs, and Architecture. The Department remains in the north wing along 77th Street, which is visible on the right in this view from Central Park.

tors Alexander J. Wall and Robert W. G. Vail secured extensive photographic collections through purchase and gift. Among their acquisitions were prints and negatives by Arnold Genthe, George P. Hall & Son, Antoinette B. Hervey, Pirie MacDonald, Burr McIntosh, the New York City Board of Rapid Transit, Pach Brothers, George E. Stonebridge, and Doris Ulmann. Curator of Manuscripts Wayne Andrews and his successors sheltered the architectural archives of Cass Gilbert; McKim, Mead & White; George B. Post; and John B. Snook. Member and staff interest in the steamboat and elevated railroad eras attracted large collections in those areas. The Society also took an active role in recording New York City history for posterity by assigning its own photographer to document local streets and buildings (Cover illustration).

The flood of new material was overwhelming.[3] In 1959, the library adopted a narrower acquisition policy to focus on material about New York City and New York State and on general American history only through the Civil War. Collection responsibilities also shifted. Most original watercolor and pen and ink drawings were transferred to the Museum around 1960. By 1970, broadsides and maps had been moved to the Library's Reading Room department, and most architectural and bookplate collections were consolidated in what was then called the Print Room. During the 1960s and 1970s, staff concentrated on historical prints. Major benefactors included antiquarian collector C. Otto von Kienbusch, Society Presidents Irving S. Olds and Robert G. Goelet, and Society Trustee Hall Park McCullough. Photographs and ephemera were featured in exhibits and books by Curator of Painting and Sculpture Mary Black, including *Old New York in Early Photographs* and *American Advertising Posters of the Nineteenth Century* from the Bella C. Landauer collection.

During the 1980s, acquisitions focused on choice individual pieces and small cohesive collections—for example, drawings by early Brooklyn architect James S. Martens, vintage prints and negatives by talented amateur Robert L. Bracklow (Figure 11), and rare historical engravings and lithographs. Staff attention also turned to programs for general preservation and cataloging. In 1989, during a major Society reorganization, the Print Room was transferred from the Library to the Museum and given a new name to better describe its scope: the Department of Prints, Photographs, and Architecture. Today, the Department continues to serve many people a year, with a curator for each main collection area and several general assistants.

---

[3] For example, the 1950 annual report lists the following additions: 3,341 bookplates; 274 trade and other cards; 1,451 broadsides and posters; 29 calendars; 46 cartoons; 52 certificates; 302 drawings and watercolors; 5 sketchbooks; 800 engravings, lithographs, and other prints; 373 postcards; 4 copperplates; 4 wood blocks; 23 daguerreotypes and tintypes; 66 lantern slides; 64,812 photographs; 40,154 photographic negatives; and 4 stereographs.

The preceding chronology summarizes acquisition trends and benchmark changes at the Society that have influenced the nature of the collections. The following overview of the current collection arrangement explains how the collections fit together and indicates their strengths within five broad areas: General, Photographs, Architecture, Prints, and Ephemera (Table 1).

Table 1. Collection Chart

■ **GENERAL**
  Geographic
  Negative
  Portrait
  Subject

■ **PHOTOGRAPHS:**
by photographer
  Albok
  Beals
  Bracklow
  Browning
  Chapman
  Genthe
  Hall
  Hewitt and Smith
  Ingalls
  Kilmer
  Lawrence
  Levick
  Liberman
  MacDonald
  McIntosh
  McLaughlin Air Service
  Photographer File
  Prevost
  Riis
  Smith
  Smyth
  Stonebridge
  Trappan
  Ulmann
  Wenzel

■ **PHOTOGRAPHS:**
by topic/collector
  Billboard
  Cathedral of St. John the Divine
  Fifth Ave. Coach Co.
  Green (elevated railroads)
  Light (New York City)
  Lighthouse
  McLaughlin Air Service
  Murdock (steamboats)
  NYHS Archive
  Penn Station
  Scanlon (steamboats)
  Silver (store displays)
  Smith (springs & wells)
  Smyth (fires)
  Subway
  Weisman (buildings)

■ **PHOTOGRAPHS:**
by format
  Album
  Carte de visite
  Cased
  Negative
  Stereograph
  Transparency

■ **ARCHITECTURE:**
by architect
  Architect & Engineer
  Davis
  Gilbert
  McComb
  McKim, Mead & White
  Pollard
  Post
  Snook

■ **ARCHITECTURE:**
by topic/collector
  Cathedral of St. John the Divine
  Geographic
  Green (elevated railroads)
  Hewitt and Smith (residences)
  Lighthouse
  McLaughlin Air Service
  Penn Station
  Silver (store displays)
  Subway

■ **PRINTS:**
by creator/collector
  Boyd (New York City)
  Havemeyer (portraits)
  Hyde (allegories)
  Keppler
  LeBoeuf (Robert Fulton)
  Liberman (Wall St.)
  Olds (naval)
  Peters (illustrated newspapers)
  Strobridge
  Wright

■ **PRINTS:**
by format
  Bookplate
  Caricature
  Certificate
  Poster
  Printing Plate
  Printmaker

■ **EPHEMERA**
  Bookplate
  Certificate
  Dorsey
  Graphic Arts
  Landauer (advertising)
  Postcard
  Poster
  Strobridge

Figure 11. Robert L. Bracklow with camera, ca. 1910. Print by Alexander Alland, ca. 1950, from negative by unidentified photographer. (Bracklow Collection, neg. no. 60851)

It can take many years to acquire a collection. Around 1950, the high quality views taken by gifted amateur photographer Robert Bracklow from the 1880s to 1910s impressed the Society so much that it bought more than 500 modern prints made by Alexander Alland from Bracklow's original negatives. In the 1980s, the Society acquired the surviving glass plate negatives and, from a separate source, wonderful albums of vintage prints. This portrait of Bracklow (1849–1919) shows the kind of large-format camera he used to create his compelling photographs of people and places.

Figure 12. Liberty's arm in Madison Square Park, Fifth Avenue, New York City. Photograph by unidentified photographer, ca. 1880. (Geographic File, neg. no. 49251)

When you need to check quickly for previously published or readily reproduced pictures, start with the Negative File's catalog. The original print of this photograph is filed under "Fifth Avenue," seen in the center. But the image is usually requested because of its special subject. At the right, the Statue of Liberty arm and torch rise from Madison Square Park. This part of the statue, after display at the 1876 Centennial Exposition (Philadelphia), was placed temporarily in the park to raise money for the full figure, completed in 1886. The view also might be indexed under gas street lights or the Worth Monument obelisk. The left corner of the original glass negative broke off and appears as a black area.

The most frequent request, "Do you have a picture of …?," is answered by consulting the basic files common to many historical repositories—the Geographic, Portrait, and Subject files. As prints and photographs arrive, staff sort many of them into these files according to place, sitter, or historical event. The files provide direct access to the primary topics shown in more than 120,000 images. There is, however, no associated catalog to provide access to other image characteristics such as artist, photographer, medium, or secondary topics. For example, researchers interested in locating works in these files *by* a particular printmaker must first compile a list of likely subjects, then look through appropriate file categories to determine what is available.

The Negative File is another basic starting point for many requests. It contains more than 80,000 original and copy negatives, most of which have been indexed by subject and, since the 1970s, by artist or photographer. The copy negatives include photographs of broadsides, maps, furniture, paintings, and other material in many Society departments. The File is, in fact, the first place to check for the Society's best known and previously published images, because negatives usually exist for those items (Figure 12).

Researchers who need to delve further can turn to the special collections and files, which fall into four areas: photographs, architecture, prints, and ephemera. The **PHOTOGRAPH COLLECTIONS** number more than 130,000 images and are especially strong in portraits and views from the 1850s to the 1930s. The special format files for albums, cartes de visite, cased photographs, negatives, stereographs, and transparencies include such landmarks in photographic history as Civil War scenes published by Mathew Brady and examples of the first American stereographs taken by the Langenheim Brothers. Among the daguerreotype treasures are a vivid portrait of statesman Henry Clay and a Crystal Palace view (Figure 13). Master photographers Andreas Feininger, Arnold Genthe (Figure 14), Victor Prevost, and Doris Ulmann are represented by substantial bodies of their work. Selected images by contemporary art photographers are in the Photographer File.

Figure 13. Crystal Palace, interior view toward the south nave and 40th Street, New York City. Daguerreotype by unidentified photographer, 1853 or 1854. (Cased Photograph File, Neg. no. 36561)

Views of building interiors are far less common than street scenes. This rare daguerreotype captures the Crystal Palace sculpture display in gleaming yet mysterious detail. (It is shown here without the original cover glass and case designed to protect the fragile image surface from damage.) The success of the 1851 London Crystal Palace inspired New Yorkers to host the first World's Fair held in the United States, called "Exhibition of the Industry of All Nations." Georg J. B. Carstensen and Charles Gildemeister designed this glass and cast-iron exhibition hall in the shape of a Greek cross. The fair ran from 1853 to 1854 in Manhattan. Reportedly fireproof, the Crystal Palace caught fire in 1858 and collapsed rapidly.

Documentary images of New York-area buildings and street life are preserved in separate collections by commercial photographers Jessie Tarbox Beals, Irving Browning, George P. Hall, Edwin Levick, and McLaughlin Air Service. Similar subjects, as well as more informal family scenes, are recorded in collections by skilled amateur photographers including John Albok, Robert L. Bracklow, Arthur D. Chapman, Frank M. Ingalls, Richard H. Lawrence, George E. Stonebridge, John J. Trappan, and Edward Wenzel. Collections with a special subject focus include steamboat and ferry photographs gathered by George W. Murdock and by Joseph Scanlon, fire photographs by Frederick H. Smyth, photographs of springs and wells by James Reuel Smith, the Billboard Photograph Collection, the Fifth Avenue Coach Co. Collection, a group of early Union Square street scenes donated by William E. Light, and a set of reference prints made from Jacob Riis' negatives. High society portraits predominate in the Burr McIntosh Collection, and there are two collections of portraits of men taken by noted professional photographer Pirie MacDonald and by amateur Theron W. Kilmer.

Several architectural photograph collections complement the architectural drawing collections. The Mattie E. Hewitt and Richard A. Smith Collection shows New York City interiors in the mid-1900s. The Silver & Company Collection features retail store interiors during the same time period. The Cathedral Church of St. John the Divine appears in construction photographs by pictorialist Antoinette B. Hervey. Alexander Hatos documents a landmark's destruction in the Pennsylvania Station Demolition Photograph Collection. The Liberman Collection photographs depict each house of worship in Manhattan in the 1970s. The Subway Collection records the New York subway system construction and buildings along its routes. The Green Collection preserves detailed views, commissioned by Society Trustee Norvin H. Green, of the dismantling of New York's elevated railroads. Turn-of-the-century lighthouses are recorded in the Lighthouse Collection. The Weisman Collection documents cast-iron architecture, skyscrapers, and commercial buildings in New York and other cities.

◄ Figure 14. Edna St. Vincent Millay at Mitchell Kennerley's house in Mamaroneck, New York. Photograph by Arnold Genthe, 1913 or 1914. (Genthe Collection, neg. no. 70808)

In addition to striking images by amateur, commercial, and unidentified photographers, the Society's collections offer prints by master artists such as Arnold Genthe (1869–1942). Genthe drew on classic, picturesque, and Oriental traditions to create beautiful soft-focus portraits and documentary views. For this scene, he posed Edna St. Vincent Millay (1892–1950), a young and newly acclaimed poet, with a blooming magnolia tree.

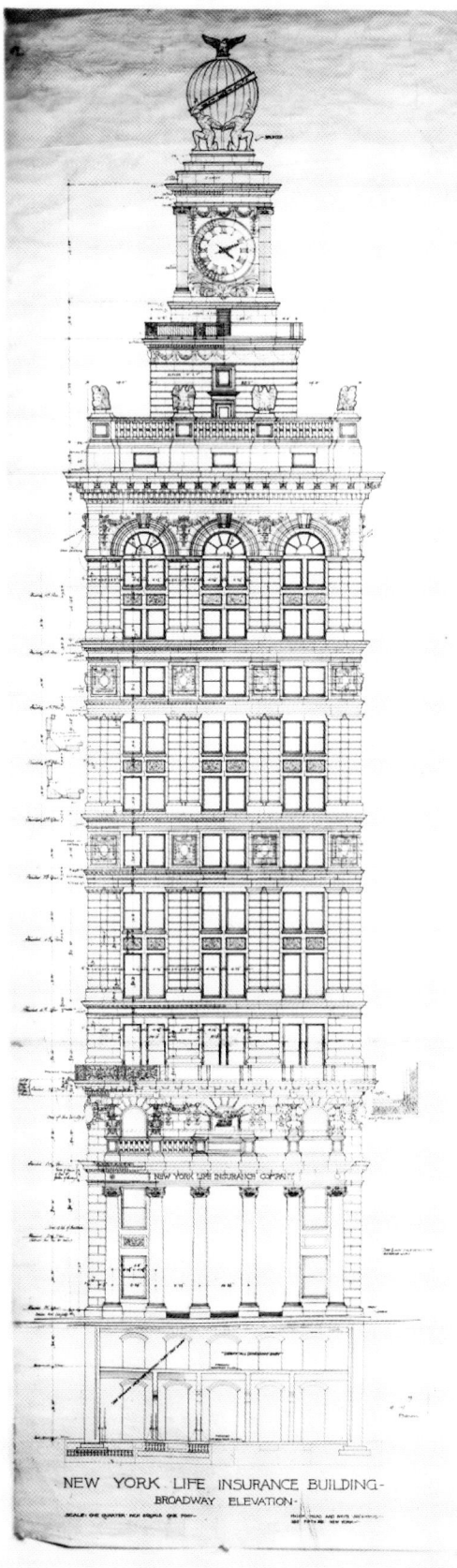

Figure 15. *New York Life Insurance Building, Broadway Elevation.* Ink drawing, ca. 1890s. (McKim, Mead & White Architectural Record Collection, neg. no. 57504)

Architectural archives are a special strength of the Society's research collections. They support aesthetic, technological, economic, political, and sociological studies because they provide thorough records: correspondence, specifications, contracts, scrapbooks, and photographs, as well as extensive sets of preliminary and finished design drawings. One of the best-known is the McKim, Mead & White Architectural Record Collection. This long drawing shows the firm's proposed extension and remodeling of an insurance company's headquarters at 346 Broadway, New York City.

The **ARCHITECTURE COLLECTIONS** contain about 130,000 drawings, blueprints, renderings, and photographs. Treasures in the Architect and Engineer File include drawings in an album of sketches compiled by John Trumbull and plans for the Gilbert Elevated Railway. Several large groups of material focus on individual architects and also represent major stages in the development of professional architecture in the United States through the early 1920s. There are, in chronological order, collections for John McComb, Jr., best known for the New York City Hall; Calvin Pollard, a builder-architect of houses, churches, and stores; Alexander J. Davis, an influential designer of residences and public buildings; John B. Snook, noted for cast-iron structures; George B. Post, who created early skyscrapers; McKim, Mead & White, famed for classical residences and public buildings (Figure 15); and Cass Gilbert, noted for such projects as the Woolworth Building. The architects were all active in Manhattan, and New York City buildings predominate, but their work includes many structures outside the City. The largest archives also contain extensive correspondence and scrapbook material, which further document projects and their designers.

Figure 16. *The Four Indian Kings.* Mezzotint by Bernard Lens, Sr., after the original limnings drawn from life by Bernard Lens, Jr., London, 1710. (Subject File, neg. no. 58228)

The Society has many historical prints from the 1700s and early 1800s that are highly valued because relatively few pictures were made in that era and even fewer copies have survived. This rare British mezzotint portrays four Iroquois sachems dressed in a mixture of Indian and European attire. Great Britain invited the men to the court of Queen Anne in 1710 to encourage the Iroqouis to fight the French, who were attacking Britain's American colonies. Tee Yee Neen Ho Ga Row, also known as Hendrick, became a famous leader of the Mohawk people.

The PRINT COLLECTIONS include almost 25,000 engravings, etchings, woodcuts, and lithographs, with special concentrations of early American engravings and lithographs supplemented by several thousand European views of American life (Figure 16). Notable printmakers represented extensively in the Printmaker File include Alexander Anderson, William J. Bennett, Robert Havell, John Hill, Anthony Imbert, and the Mavericks. The experimental prints by Arthur J. Stansbury are thought to be the first lithographs printed in New York. The Printing Plate File documents the printmaking process through lithographic stones, copper engraving plates, and photomechanical blocks. The Wright Collection also documents printing history with numerous photomechanical specimens by commercial pioneer Charles Lennox Wright.

The Caricature File provides an outstanding survey of American political and social prints and drawings from the 1700s to the early 1900s. The Keppler Collection features cartoons by Joseph Keppler, the founder of *Puck*, and by his son. Newsworthy events and individuals are also portrayed in the Peters Collection in thousands of wood engravings from illustrated newspapers of the 1840s to the early 1900s. The Havemeyer Collection provides many commercial printing specimens in its portraits of American statesmen. The Olds Collection and LeBoeuf Collection feature views of pre-Civil War naval engagements and vessels and portraits of naval heroes, printed in Britain and France as well as in the United States. The allegorical prints in the Hyde Collection record European impressions of the Americas as a rich and exotic territory to conquer. In contrast to the bulk of the collections, which are historical prints, the Boyd Collection provides artists' representations of New York City from the 1920s to the present. The Liberman Collection of Wall Street prints contains similar material on that single theme.

The **EPHEMERA COLLECTIONS** offer almost 500,000 lottery tickets, speakeasy cards, billheads, tobacco labels, paper roses, and countless other types of material that were created for temporary use but have survived to illuminate everyday life and popular culture. The Landauer Collection, one of the largest ephemera treasure troves in the United States, features business papers and social souvenirs from the 1700s to early 1900s and provides a colorful overview of advertising techniques (Figure 17). The Dorsey Collection offers scrapbooks of engravings, illustrations, and ephemera organized around such themes as expositions, hotels, and New York City. The Graphic Arts File contains substantial groups of clipper ship sailing cards, pictorial stationery, patriotic envelopes, and fraktur illuminations. So many bookplates, certificates, postcards, and posters were received from different sources that they have been organized into separate files. The Certificate and Bookplate files provide many examples of early American engraving and design. The Postcard File documents local views and events, sometimes with enlivening comments from the correspondents. The Poster File is strong in book and magazine placards, entertainment posters, and World War I and World War II government posters. Close to 1,000 circus and theatrical posters are also in the Strobridge Collection.

Collections in one department of the Society often complement those in other areas. I.N. Phelps Stokes, for example, relied heavily on the Society's manuscript, map, and local history materi-

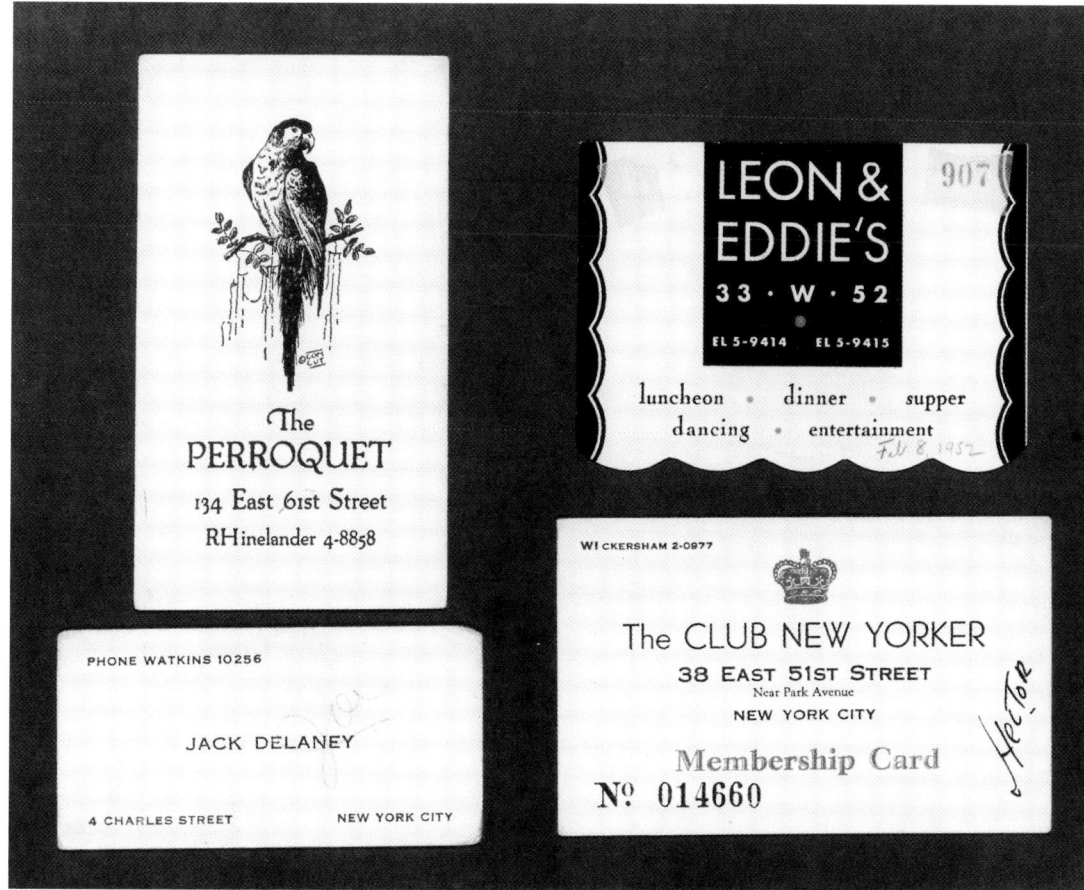

Figure 17. Speakeasy cards, 1920s. (Landauer Collection, neg. no. 49992)

Among the Society's prized holdings are ephemeral documents of life in New York City, including numerous speakeasy cards, which were used to gain entrance to nightclubs during Prohibition. The Eighteenth Amendment made the manufacture, sale, and transport of alcoholic beverages illegal between 1920 and 1933. Thousands of speakeasies opened in different parts of New York, including many in Manhattan's midtown area, mentioned on several of the cards shown here.

als while compiling his monumental *Iconography of Manhattan*. The 700,000-volume Library offers outstanding reference sources critical to the interpretation of pictorial materials, including fire insurance maps, city directories, long runs of local newspapers, travel accounts, regimental histories, and naval histories. Diaries, account books, and correspondence in the Manuscript Department are also valuable for investigating the creators and subjects of visual materials. The Society Archives provides acquisition records and correspondence with donors that may help interpret a collection.

Many visual materials are available in other departments. The Department of Paintings, Sculpture, and Decorative Arts has thousands of oil portraits, watercolor drawings, statues, medals, silverware, and other objects. Most broadsides, theatrical playbills, sheet music, menus, greeting cards, and trade catalogs are in the Library (as well as in the Landauer Collection). The Library has many illustrated books, which can provide images not available in the Department of Prints, Photographs, and Architecture. The Manuscript Department also has pictorial documents, most notably in sets of books which were extra-illustrated through the addition of autographed letters, portrait engravings, lithographic views, and even original drawings. Small numbers of family photographs are sometimes retained in the family papers.

Special collections are usually divided among departments according to format. For example, the Robert Fulton books, letters, paintings, and prints in the LeBoeuf Collection have been dispersed so that materials are in the care of the department best prepared to handle them. Textual records of the American Art Union are in the Manuscript Department, and the prints published for its subscribers are in the Printmaker File. After almost 200 years of collecting activity, material sought from unrelated sources often fits well together. For example, the Society bought John James Audubon's original watercolors for *The Birds of America* in 1863, received the printed double elephant folio edition as a gift in the 1950s, and purchased a rare Audubon lithograph of clapper rails in the 1980s. It is also possible to study the design development and printing technique of several printmakers, including Anderson and Bennett (Figure 18), because the Society has in its various departments examples of several stages of their work—from original drawings and correspondence to printing plates and final prints.

Figure 18. *South St. from Maiden Lane.* Aquatint engraved by William J. Bennett, published by Henry J. Megarey, New York, 1828. (Printmaker File, neg. no. 29513)

By itself, this master print documents Manhattan's lively maritime commerce in the early 1800s. Together with the Society's other prints and drawings by William James Bennett (ca. 1784-1844), this aquatint provides an opportunity to study Bennett's work in depth.

Preparation of the guide

A collection guide was proposed in 1981 as a first step in unifying reference access, setting preservation and cataloging priorities, focusing collection development, and making the collections better known to more research communities. The initial collection survey resembled a treasure hunt. After compiling a list of major acquisitions from annual reports and from *Knickerbocker Birthday* (the Society's sesquicentennial history), staff inventoried the Print Room's eight storage areas. Long-separated materials were reunited and mysterious indexes were deciphered. Fifteen new collections were identified and added to the core of 35 collections that had been in regular use for many years. The survey established file names; estimated quantities of material, date ranges, and subject strengths; and assessed arrangement patterns, indexes, and physical conditions. By 1983, enough information had been compiled to produce an in-house guide with preliminary descriptions of 50 collections.

The survey stimulated cataloging. During the next eight years, information in the in-house guide was expanded by examining collections in greater detail and compiling preliminary finding aids. Twenty-four additional collections were sorted and described, and several collections were rehoused in suitable folders and boxes. In the 1990s, efforts focused on improving access through cataloging and making ready reference photocopies to enable visual browsing of large material and reduce handling of fragile original images. One extensive new collection was also cataloged. Although far more pictorial materials are now available to researchers, considerably more work is needed to store and index all of the collections in keeping with recent archival and museum standards to ensure their long-term preservation and full accessibility. Much also remains to be discovered about many individual images and several collections.

The Society has already begun a major effort to secure the necessary resources. The photograph and architecture collections, for example, now have the attention of full-time curators. Funding is being sought to process the thousands of photographs that remain to be arranged and cataloged—among them, images by or associated with Eugene L. Armbruster, George T. Bagoe, Hermann Blumenthal, Thomas J. Burton, Edmund B. Child, George C. Dodd, John Ward Dunsmore, William D. Hassler (Figure 19), Austin Baxter Keep, and the recently acquired Thomas Air Views. Other collections need preservation before they can be readily handled. Examples include rare unmounted cartes de visite and larger salt prints, probably from Mathew Brady's studio, and platinum prints of Broadway and New York City scenes by Charles Gilbert Hine.

Figure 19. Vanitie Beauty Shop, between 107th and 108th Street, New York City. Glass negative by William D. Hassler, undated. (Hassler Collection, neg. no. Hassler-4460)

While many collections are already available to the public, others such as the several hundred glass negatives attributed to William D. Hassler require additional resources so that they can be preserved and cataloged. This intriguing view shows women ready to welcome customers to what is possibly a new business in upper Manhattan. A sign on the partition advertises, "Artistic Hair Goods—Made to Order."

Organization of the Guide

The *Guide* describes all collections available for public use in 1998, and information is current through that year. There are 75 entries, arranged alphabetically by title, which describe 56 special collections and 19 general files. The word *collection* in an entry title designates groups of material received and maintained as distinct units to emphasize the special context that brought the material together and that adds to its research value. The Strobridge Poster Collection, for example, documents the history of a major lithography company and the techniques of theatrical and circus advertising as much as it depicts specific entertainments. The word *file* designates groups of pictures received from many sources and put together because of physical format storage considerations or ready reference needs. New material is continually added to the files, which have been set up for: Albums, Architects' and Engineers' works, Bookplates, Caricatures and Cartoons, Cartes de Visite, Cased Photographs, Certificates, Geographic views, Graphic Arts, Negatives, Photographers' works, Portraits, Postcards, Posters, Printmakers' works, Printing Plates, Stereographs (Figure 20), specific Subjects, and Transparencies. In the past, special collections were sometimes dispersed among the general files in order to provide subject access. Those collection names are mentioned in the appropriate *Guide* entries and in the general index.

Entries vary in length depending on the material's cohesiveness or complexity and on the amount of information compiled so far. Each entry includes several elements:

The ENTRY NUMBER is assigned according to the alphabetical order of entry names. The *Guide*'s general index refers to these entry numbers.

The COLLECTION OR FILE NAME is given in its full form. With collections, a personal or corporate name followed by a type of media indicates that the person or organization created the material, e.g., *Jessie Tarbox Beals Photograph Collection*. A personal name followed directly by the word *collection* indicates that the person assembled the material from a variety of sources, e.g., the *Harry T. Peters Collection of Pictorial Newspaper Illustrations*.

DATES refer to the time period depicted in the images rather than the years in which the material was created. Span dates are listed first and provide the earliest and latest years covered. Bulk dates identify predominant years. The abbreviation *ca. (circa)* indicates approximate years.

Figure 20. *Panorama of the Ramble, Central Park. Snow not yet melted.*
Photograph by Frederick F. Thompson, April 1862. (Stereograph File, neg. no. 58870)

The Society's noted Stereograph File includes images that document the history of photography, as well as specific subjects. This view of the Ramble and Bow Bridge depicts a then-new area of Manhattan's Central Park, which opened in 1859. It is also a rare example of early efforts to master the difficult-to-handle wet plate negative techniques and the special stereoscopic format. The photographer, Frederick F. Thompson was a Wall Street banker who belonged to the Amateur Photographic Exchange Club. Members in different cities printed and circulated their stereograph cards to share technical information.

The **PHYSICAL DESCRIPTION AREA** states the quantity and type of material. Most amounts are estimates, marked by the abbreviation *ca.* and rounded to the nearest 50, 100, or 1,000 count. General terminology is used to identify media when a collection contains a variety of processes or when more investigation is needed to determine specific processes. Dimensions are given only when material falls within a small range of sizes. Accompanying items that provide background information, such as a photographer's logbooks, are mentioned last.

The **SCOPE NOTE** begins with general statements about the type of material, the creator's career, or the collector's intent. The remainder of the note describes the Society's holdings with an emphasis on the chief or representative subject matter, potential research value, and nature of captions. So many of the collections concern New York

City that an effort has been made to convey the flavor and quality of material through more subjective descriptions than are usually found in collection guides.

The **ARRANGEMENT AND ACCESS NOTE** describes the material's physical filing order and the access provided by indexes, checklists, and other finding aids at the Society, many of which are preliminary inventories. The type of arrangement (alphabetical, geographical, chronological, topical, or numerical) and the degree of indexing affect the amount of information a researcher must be prepared to provide and the amount of time necessary to answer a particular query. For example, a researcher seeking information about Niagara Falls bridges might be more easily served by a geographically arranged file of New York State views than by a chronological file of bridges. Material still being processed is mentioned only in the description area and scope note, and staff should be consulted about its availability.

A **PROVENANCE NOTE** lists the immediate source of acquisition, when it is known. This note is not provided for files, because they contain material from many sources.

A **RESTRICTIONS NOTE** identifies major copyright or donor limitations on use of the collection. Additional restrictions that apply to individual images may be found with the material.

A **REFERENCES NOTE** cites substantive published descriptions of the material.

A **RELATED NOTE** refers to similar material elsewhere in the Society.

An **AT OTHER INSTITUTIONS NOTE** refers to closely related material in other repositories that are open to the public (Figure 21).

There are two indexes. The **CHRONOLOGICAL INDEX** displays each collection's span and bulk dates to aid researchers interested in whatever images are available about a particular time period. The **GENERAL INDEX** provides access to key creators, subjects, places, media, formats, and collection names and to each illustration. Images mentioned merely to indicate a file's content are not indexed. More exhaustive indexing is often available in finding aids. The **BIBLIOGRAPHY** lists publications about material in more than one collection. Major catalogs of collections with pictorial material in other departments are also included. Published descriptions of individual collections are

Figure 21. *Miss Duray Leonora.* Barnum & Bailey circus poster. Chromolithograph by Strobridge Lithographing Company, Cincinnati, New York, and London, ca. 1900. (Strobridge Collection, neg. no. 63984)

Some archives are shared among several institutions. The New-York Historical Society has about 1,000 circus and theatrical posters, plus photographs and drawings from the Strobridge Lithographing Company, which was based in Cincinnati, Ohio. The Cincinnati Historical Society has the firm's account books, correspondence, and other records. In this exuberant scene, the different views of Miss Duray Leonora's contortions resemble the mental dexterity sometimes needed for successful picture research. The rewards, however, are worth the effort.

listed with the appropriate entries. The ILLUSTRATIONS usually represent collection strengths. More than 30 are being published here for the first time. An effort has been made to show the entire image, but some photos have been slightly cropped. Each caption includes an original title (in italics) or a devised title; readily available information about the medium, creator, and date; and the negative number from which copies can be ordered.

Public services

Staff provides reference assistance in response to phone or mail inquiries, but most research must be conducted by visiting the Society. Researchers should telephone the Society before visiting to verify hours and staff availability. Each researcher is asked to exercise special care in handling the inherently fragile images and to consult reference copies, rather than original materials, whenever such copies are available. All material must be used in the Department. Staff will make xerographic copies of images that can be safely photocopied, at a nominal cost. The Department has numerous reference books to help interpret its collections. There are also several specialized indexes to help researchers locate selected materials regardless of their filing category: Artist and Engraver Index, Lithographer and Publisher Index, and Photographer Index. For more information contact:

>Department of Prints, Photographs, and Architecture
>The New-York Historical Society
>170 Central Park West
>New York, New York 10024-5194
>(212) 873-3400

The Department of Rights and Reproductions provides photoduplication services by selling several types of black-and-white and color photographs. A price list is available on request. Fees for nonprofit and commercial publication are additional, and publication permission must be requested. The Society observes the canons of fair use in duplicating material, but responsibility for use of the copies rests with the purchaser. All reproductions must be accompanied by the credit line:

"Courtesy of The New-York Historical Society, New York City."

Bibliography

The following books and articles describe or reproduce visual material in several of the Society's collections. A few general Society histories and reports are also included. Publications that focus on a single collection are listed with the entry for that collection.

Architectural Research Materials in New York City. New York: Committee for the Preservation of Architectural Records, 1977.

Black, Mary, comp. *Old New York in Early Photographs, 1853-1901: 196 Prints from the Collection of The New-York Historical Society.* 2d rev. ed. New York: Dover, 1976.

Blom, Benjamin. *New York Photographs, 1850-1950.* New York: E.P. Dutton, 1982.

Breton, Arthur J. *Guide to the Manuscript Collections of The New-York Historical Society.* 2 vols. Westport, Conn.: Greenwood Press, 1972.

Chicago and New York: Architectural Interactions. Chicago: Art Institute of Chicago, 1984.

Davidson, Marshall B. *New York: A Pictorial History.* New York: Scribners, 1977.

Eskind, Andrew H., and Greg Drake, eds. *Index to American Photographic Collections.* 2d enl. ed. Boston: G.K. Hall, 1990.

Guthrie, Kevin M. *The New-York Historical Society: Lessons from One Nonprofit's Long Struggle for Survival.* San Francisco: Jossey-Bass Publishers, 1996.

Heslin, James J. "Library Acquisition Policy of The New-York Historical Society." *The New-York Historical Society Quarterly* 46 (Jan. 1962): 87-106.

"Images of American Life." *Occasional Observer: A Newsletter of The New-York Historical Society* (Fall 1977).

Jackson, Kenneth T., ed. *The Encyclopedia of New York City.* New Haven, Conn.: Yale University Press; New York: The New-York Historical Society, 1995.

Koke, Richard J., comp. *American Landscape and Genre Paintings in The New-York Historical Society: A Catalog of the Collection, Including Historical, Narrative, and Marine Art.* 3 vols. New York: The New-York Historical Society; Boston: G.K. Hall, 1982.

Kouwenhoven, John. *Columbia Historical Portrait of New York.* Garden City, N.Y.: Doubleday, 1953.

Mayor, A. Hyatt. *Popular Prints of the Americas.* New York: Crown, 1973.

The New-York Historical Society. *Annual Report of the Committee on the Fine Arts.* 1862.

The New-York Historical Society. *Catalogue of American Portraits in The New-York Historical Society.* 2 vols. New Haven, Conn.: Yale University Press, 1974.

The New-York Historical Society. *Quarterly.* 1917-1980, vols. 1-64.

Richards, Pamela S. *Scholars and Gentlemen: The Library of The New-York Historical Society, 1804-1982.* Hamden, Conn.: Archon, 1984. (Does not discuss the Print Room.)

Shadwell, Wendy. "Commercial and Job Printing Serving the Maritime Industries." In *American Maritime Prints: Proceedings of the Eighth Annual North American Print Conference, 1977,* ed. by Elton W. Hall. New Bedford, Mass.: Old Dartmouth Historical Society, 1985, pp. 95-129.

Shadwell, Wendy. "Pictorial Ephemera in The New-York Historical Society." *PictureScope* 31 (Summer 1983): 44-49.

Shadwell, Wendy. "Prized Prints: Rare American Prints Before 1860 in the Collection of The New-York Historical Society." *Imprint* 11 (Spring 1986): 1-27.

Stern, Robert A.M., et al. *New York 1900: Metropolitan Architecture and Urbanism, 1890-1915.* New York: Rizzoli, 1983.

Stokes, Isaac Newton Phelps. *The Iconography of Manhattan Island, 1498-1909.* 6 vols. New York: R.H. Dodd, 1915-1928.

Sullivan, Larry E. "The Print Collections of The New-York Historical Society." *Imprint* 6 (Autumn 1981): 20-24.

Vail, R.W.G. *Knickerbocker Birthday: A Sesqui-centennial History of The New-York Historical Society, 1804-1954.* New York: The New-York Historical Society, 1954.

Vail, R.W.G. "Gold Fever: A Catalogue of the California Gold Rush Centennial Exhibition." *The New-York Historical Society Quarterly* 33 (Oct. 1949): 236-271.

Wall, Alexander J., Jr. "The Story of Photography in America." *The New-York Historical Society Quarterly* 23 (October 1939): 124-130.

Zinkham, Helena. "Pungent Salt: Mathew Brady's 1866 Negotiations with The New-York Historical Society." *History of Photography* 10 (Jan.-March 1986): 1-8.

The Collections

The Collections

Figure 22. General view of New York World's Fair, Flushing Meadows, Queens. Gelatin silver print by John Albok, 1939. (Neg. no. 64822)

The photograph shows (from left) the Fair's futuristic symbol called the Trylon and Perisphere, the hemispherical U.S. Steel Building, and Carrier Corporation's cone-shaped pavilion at which air conditioning was demonstrated.

1. JOHN ALBOK PHOTOGRAPH COLLECTION
ca. 1928-1980, bulk 1930s-1960s.
ca. 1,000 photographic prints (most 8 × 10 in.) and 1,500 film negatives (2 1/4 × 2 1/4 in. and 5 × 7 in.).

Hungarian-born John Albok (1894-1982) immigrated to the United States in 1921 and opened a small tailor shop on upper Madison Avenue in Manhattan, New York. His store also served as his photographic studio. For 60 years, Albok documented city life and won recognition for his ability to portray people's inherent dignity and to find beauty in an urban environment. He created an archive estimated at 15,000 prints. The Society's portion of the archive includes many images of Central Park scenery, the 1939-1940 World's Fair (Figure 22), World War II rallies, ethnic parades, and street scenes.

Arrangement and access: Most prints are filed by date.
Restrictions: Permission to reproduce the photographs must be obtained from the donor.
Provenance: Gift from the photographer's daughter, Ilona Albok Vitarius, in 1984-1997.

Figure 23. General Tom Thumb (Charles Stratton) and his wife Lavinia Warren, posed with a baby. Carte de visite attributed to Mathew Brady's studio, ca. 1865.
(Neg. no. 36919)

General Tom Thumb (1838-1883) began his performing career as a child at P.T. Barnum's museum in New York City. His small size and lively manner made him an international celebrity. He grew to a height just over three feet and married Lavinia Warren in 1863.

2. ALBUM FILE

ca. 1800-present, bulk 1850s-1950s.
ca. 410 volumes: chiefly photographs; also, some prints, clippings, and ephemera.

The Album File contains unpublished volumes of pictures. Topics and formats vary widely, but photographic portraits of local and national figures predominate. Albums of special interest include *Historical Portraits,* a rare 28-volume set of carte de visite-size photographs printed in the 1910s by Frederick Hill Meserve from negatives taken in the 1800s chiefly by the Mathew Brady studio. It features some 8,000 notable people arranged by occupation, and an entire volume is devoted to Abraham Lincoln. (Many of the corresponding negatives are now at the National Portrait Gallery.) Albums that belonged to the Countess Magri, the former Mrs. Tom Thumb, also feature well-known personalities (Figure 23). Formal photographic yearbooks from the 1860s and later portray New York State legislators and students at the United States Military Academy (West Point), at Dartmouth College, and at Packard Business College. A loving chronicle of family activities, 1890s-1920s, appears in several volumes filled by gifted amateur Howard M. Canoune (Introduction, Figure 1). People in other family albums are not always identified by name, but their portraits may be of interest from a costume, photographic, or social history point of view.

Geographic view albums depict New York City construction projects, business and residential interiors, and such civic celebrations as the subway opening in Manhattan. One volume, possibly a salesman's sample stock, contains halves of New York City stereograph views sold by E. & H.T. Anthony in 1867. For pictorial histories, Reginald P. Bolton gathered views of Washington Heights; Thomas F. DeVoe and George A. Zabriskie illustrated New York City history through clippings from books and periodicals. Amateur vacation views record an 1891-1892 tour of western states (captured with an early handheld Kodak camera), the 1901 Buffalo Pan-American Exposition, and camp-

Figure 24. Ambulance drill with Zouaves, at headquarters of the Army of the Potomac near Brandy Station, Virginia, March, 1864. Print by unidentified photographer in *Photographs of the War of Rebellion*, vol. 5, pl. 47. (Neg. no. 53563)

ing in the Adirondack Mountains. Foreign travel volumes often include commercially sold photographs. For example, tourist views of Havana, Cuba, appear in Oswald H. Ernst's album from ca. 1900.

Another prized set of albums is the 31-volume *Photographs of the War of Rebellion* (Figure 24). It provides several thousand Civil War scenes and portraits, which were printed from negatives associated with Mathew Brady, E. & H.T. Anthony, and Alexander Gardner (and are now at the Library of Congress). A collector's display book of 120 carte de visite caricature photographs also dates from the Civil War.

Arrangement and access: Albums are filed by sequentially assigned numbers. A card index has been started to list each album by its date, with a short description and cross references under broad categories (e.g., Portraits—Richards Family; Geographic—Cuba; Subjects—Costumes) and under pictorial formats (e.g., Cabinet cards). Primary photographers are listed in the Photographer Reference Index. The two large album sets have their own indexes.

References: Christopher Gray, "A Very Special Family Album," *Avenue* 7 (May 1983): 58-67. Describes the Canoune albums.

Related: Albums are also kept with other collections, and most can be located through the index to this guide. Small souvenir viewbooks published by Wittemann Brothers, the Albertype Company, and others are in the Geographic File. Most print and photograph albums published as books, such as Alexander Gardner's *Photographic Sketch Book of the Civil War*, are in the Reading Room collections. Both the Reading Room and Manuscript Department have many collections that include scrapbooks with pictures.

Figure 25. *Plan of Arch and Truss for the Gilbert Elevated Railway, New York.* Ink and watercolor drawing by C.L. Cooke, Civil Engineer, ca. 1875. (Neg. no. 64106)

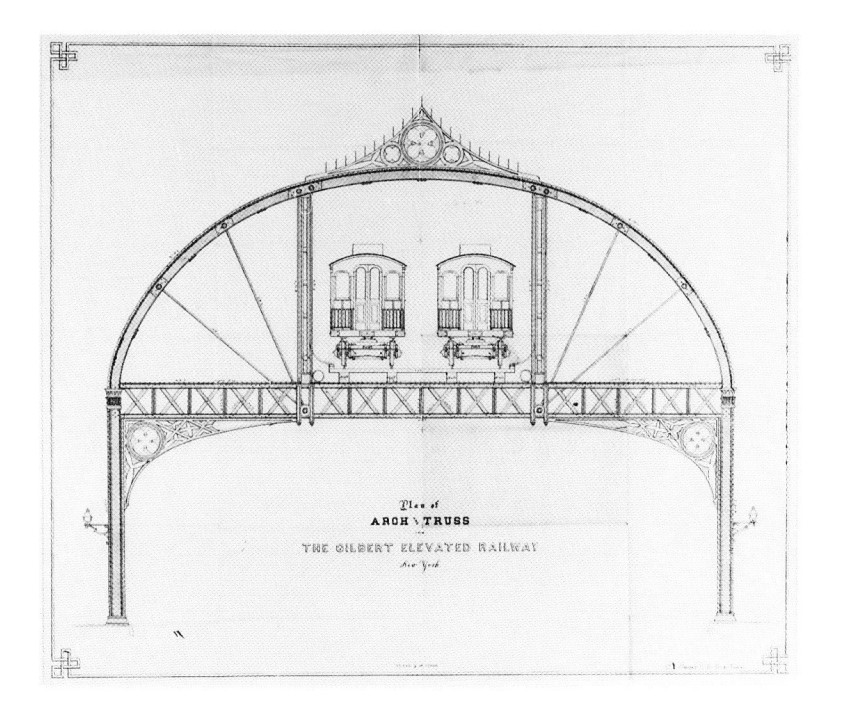

3. ARCHITECT AND ENGINEER FILE

ca. 1800-present, bulk 1850s-1930s.
More than 1,500 architectural and engineering drawings in many media, including ink and graphite drawings, renderings, sketches, blueprints, and lithographs; also, more than 1,500 photographs.

Works by more than 80 locally and nationally prominent architects and engineers are represented. Although most projects are in the New York City region, the file has such diverse material as: an album of ideal houses and U.S. Capitol drawings by John Trumbull, ca. 1800–1820; engineering schemes for the Gilbert Elevated Railway, ca. 1875 (Figure 25); estate landscaping plans by Schermerhorn & Foulks, ca. 1910; and designs for structures on Long Island by Christian F. Rosborg, 1920s–1930s. Well-known designers include Charles Bulfinch; Carrère & Hastings; Ernest Flagg; John Haviland; Peabody & Stearns; James Renwick, Jr.; William Strickland; Richard Upjohn; Calvert Vaux; and Warren & Wetmore. There are usually fewer than 10 drawings by any one architect, but a recent donation added more than 100 residential elevations, floor plans, and ornamental detail sketches made ca. 1850 by Brooklyn architect James W. Martens. The file also contains photographs, taken in the early to mid-1900s, of buildings by Delano & Aldrich, Raymond M. Hood, and Arthur B. Jennings.

Arrangement and access: Most material is filed by the designer's name; unattributed work is filed by project name or building type. A card index provides a brief description under the designer's name and sometimes under project name. It includes cross references for names of architects and engineers represented in other collections and in the Manuscript Department.

References: Holdings have been reported to the National Union Index to Architectural Records at the Library of Congress. Most of the architects are listed in: *Architectural Research Materials in New York City* (New York: Committee for the Preservation of Architectural Records, 1977).

Related: Works by Alexander J. Davis; Cass Gilbert; John McComb; McKim, Mead & White; Calvin Pollard; George B. Post; and John B. Snook are described in separate entries. Naval architecture blueprints of Hudson River steamboats are in the Subject File. Drawings for the Society's own buildings are part of The New-York Historical Society Pictorial Archive. Architects' correspondence and some sketches are also in the Manuscript Department. Building renderings are also in the Department of Paintings, Sculpture, and Decorative Arts.

4. JESSIE TARBOX BEALS PHOTOGRAPH COLLECTION
ca. 1905–ca. 1940.
ca. 350 photographic prints (8 × 10 in. and smaller).

Jessie Tarbox Beals (1870–1942), a school teacher who taught herself photography, joined the Buffalo *Courier* staff in 1902 and became known as the first woman press photographer. She practiced many types of commercial photography with the vigor and speed associated with news work, from official photographer at the Louisiana Purchase Exposition to documentary photographer of New York slum children for the Community Service Society, garden photographer for magazines, and local portraitist. Beals opened a studio in New York in 1905 but continued to travel and publish widely. The Society's holdings include portraits of Emily Post, Tony Sarg, Mark Twain, and other artists and writers; photographic postcards and large prints of Bohemian Greenwich Village in New York City (Figure 26); and such fashion photographs as the "right way to carry a bag and umbrella." There are also views of a few gardens, architecture in Boston, scenes in Arkansas, and several portraits of Beals.

Arrangement and access: Portraits are filed alphabetically by sitter. Other prints are grouped by subject.
Provenance: Various sources.
At other institutions: The Schlesinger Library at Radcliffe College has numerous photographs by Beals and also her papers. The Frances Loeb Library at Harvard University has many of her house and garden photographs. The Rare Books and Manuscripts Library at Columbia University has the slum studies taken for the Community Service Society.

Figure 26. *Great Lurid Blobs of Color on a Wooden Box, and Bobby Edwards in his Garret 'Neath the Stars Creating Eukalalies, Greenwich Village, New York.* Photographic postcard by Jessie Tarbox Beals, ca. 1910. (Neg. no. 64184)

Figure 27. West 125th Street between Seventh Avenue and Lenox Avenue, Harlem, New York City. Film negative, by unidentified photographer, January 27, 1928. (Neg. no. 60119)

The Christensen School of Music (center building) advertises "Rag & Jazz Taught on All Instruments."

5. BILLBOARD PHOTOGRAPH COLLECTION
1919–1934.
ca. 920 negatives (250 glass and 670 film, most 8 × 10 in.); a few modern prints.

The photographs, possibly by Drucker & Baltes Co., appear to have been taken to record which advertisers bought billboard space at 13 sites in Manhattan and two sites in the Bronx, New York City. The views focus on signs but also show surrounding buildings, elevated railroads, and street activity at such heavily traveled intersections as Broadway and Seventh Avenue (Times Square), Fifth Avenue at 42nd Street, Sixth Avenue at 27th Street, Eighth Avenue at 110th Street, 125th Street in Harlem (Figure 27), and Third Avenue at 166th Street in the Bronx. The same sites appear repeatedly, sometimes monthly, during the 1920s and into the Great Depression. The photographs reveal changes in both the neighborhoods and in the advertising for many products, among them Chesterfield cigarettes, Wrigley's chewing gum, and Pepsodent toothpaste.

Arrangement and access: The negatives are filed chronologically. The finding aid indexes geographic locations and execution dates but not products advertised in the billboards. Major intersections are also referenced in the Negative File catalog. A few modern prints, made in 1982, are in the Geographic File by street address.
Provenance: Purchase in 1982.

6. BOOKPLATE FILE

1500s–present, bulk 1750s–1940s.
More than 20,000 bookplates and library labels, chiefly engravings. Accompanied by 250 books and periodicals about bookplates, and by some printing plates, portrait photographs, design drawings, and correspondence.

Bookplates often provide insight into the character of the people and organizations that commissioned them and are also of value for the study of heraldry, graphic arts, and printing history (Introduction, Figure 9). The invention of movable type in the 1400s made books more plentiful, and bookplates developed as practical ownership labels. The popularity of collecting bookplates from the late-1800s through the 1920s stimulated demand for custom designs, which were exchanged to build personal collections. The Society's file, in addition to the almost complete collections of works by renowned designers Edwin D. French, Arthur N. Macdonald, Sidney L. Smith, and J. Winfred Spenceley, includes many pre-1850 American bookplates by such engravers as Henry Dawkins and the Mavericks as well as more modern plates, such as woodcuts by Julius J. Lankes from the 1920s. Basic bookplate types and styles are well-represented: armorial, allegorical, whimsical, library interior, portrait, and simple name labels. Of particular interest are a group of bookplates engraved for New Yorkers, ca. 1790, and Bella C. Landauer's correspondence with artists and fellow collectors (**Figures 28 and 29**).

Arrangement and access: The file has nine sections. The largest is the General section, in which American and European bookplates from various sources have been interfiled with the thousands of plates donated by Oliver C. Sheean. Several other sections consist of extensive groups of plates left in the order established by their collectors: Bella C. Landauer, James W. Brown, and Henry P. de Forest. There are also separate sections for printing plates commissioned by Landauer, Sheean, and others and for books about bookplates. In most sections, plates are filed alphabetically by the name of the plate owner or artist, but some scrapbooks and boxes of loose plates are devoted to a particular nationality. Ready access to subject matter is limited to several scrapbooks that cover such themes as medicine, college, library, and theater. Since donors' interests overlapped, copies of a plate may appear in several sections of the file. Most design drawings, photographs, and correspondence are in the General, Landauer, and de Forest sections. A published finding aid describes each section's categories in some detail.

References: Helena Zinkham, "The New-York Historical Society Bookplate Collection Inventory," *Bookplates in the News,* no. 71 (Jan. 1988): 710-714. Helena Zinkham, "Lend a Hand: Bella C. Landauer Bookplates at The New-York Historical Society," *American Society of Bookplate Collectors & Designers Yearbook,* 1984, pp. 14-37.

Related: Correspondence volumes in the Landauer Collection also contain letters from bookplate designers and collectors. The Manuscript Department has Edwin D. French letters. Additional books on bookplates are in the Reading Room collections.

Figures 28 and 29. Bookplates made for Bella C. Landauer. Top: Etching proof by Sidney Lawton Smith, 1926. (Neg. no. 61276). Bottom: Color woodcut by Eüchi Hirose, 1930s. (Neg. no. 61269)

Bella C. Landauer began to collect bookplates in 1923, and her correspondence indicates that she soon commissioned bookplates from several artists she admired. Landauer chose a wide variety of styles and subjects to reflect her diverse interests. In one of her early plates, the "Lend a Hand" motto appears above an optimistic landscape, which is shown here as a proof plate before her name was added. The later bookplate is a multi-color woodcut and includes a flowering plum tree branch among its Japanese motifs.

7. JAMES BOYD COLLECTION OF NEW YORK CITY PRINTS

1880s–present, bulk 1900–1930s.
ca. 800 prints, chiefly etchings; also, lithographs, woodcuts, linoleum prints, drypoints, and other print processes. Accompanied by 20 print exhibition catalogs.

James Boyd began the collection in 1935 by donating 460 etchings of New York City in memory of his wife, Agnes Gray Boyd. Through the mid-1940s, he added etchings that feature striking buildings and pleasant aspects of city life and that were created by American artists influenced by illustrated newspaper subjects and styles. In 1980, the Society began to broaden the collection to cover a wider spectrum of subjects, time periods, and print processes. The emphasis remains on recognizable rather than highly abstract views. Most of the 110 artists are local figures. Those represented by 10 or more prints include: Gottlob L. Briem, Syd Browne, Karl Dehmann, F. Leo Hunter, William C. McNulty, Charles F.W. Mielatz (Figure 30), Edith Nankivell, Betty W. Parish, Ernest D. Roth, Anton Schutz, Paul Simonsen, William H. Wallace, Elisha K.K. Wetherill, and Charles H. White. Among recent acquisitions are 80 drypoints by Mortimer Borne and a James Penney lithograph of subway riders in 1932.

Figure 30. *Old Tom's*. Etching by Charles F.W. Mielatz, 1902–1906. (Neg. no. 46593)

Charles Frederick William Mielatz (1864–1919) often created picturesque scenes of New York City. Old Tom's tavern stood at the corner of Thames and Temple Streets in lower Manhattan.

Arrangement and access: The prints are filed by sequential numbers that indicate the order in which they were added to the collection. A card catalog provides access by artist and by one or two title key words. A set of photocopies arranged by print number is available for ready reference.

Provenance: Gift from James Boyd in 1935–1944, with additions from other sources.

Related: The Liberman Collection of Wall Street Prints includes similar works. Four canceled printing plates donated by Boyd and 10 ten plates etched by Gottlob Briem are in the Printing Plate File. The Manuscript Department has diaries by William H. Wallace. The Department of Paintings, Sculpture, and Decorative Arts has drawings and paintings by several of the represented printmakers.

Figure 31. Croton Reservoir, corner of Fifth Avenue and 42nd Street, New York City. Glass negative by Robert L. Bracklow, ca. 1895. (Neg. no. Bracklow 322-A)

New York City received its first dependable water supply when the Croton Aqueduct system opened in the 1840s. This photograph shows the massive walls of Croton's distributing reservoir, which was demolished in 1899-1900 to make room for the New York Public Library.

8. ROBERT L. BRACKLOW PHOTOGRAPH COLLECTION
1880s-1910s.
28 albums (715 prints, most platinum); ca. 650 loose prints; 8 prints mounted on cards with Bracklow's imprint; ca. 2,100 modern contact prints (5 × 7 in.) and 750 modern enlargements (8 × 10 in.); ca. 2,050 glass negatives (most 5 × 7 in.); and a few lantern slides. Accompanied by 2 photographer's logbooks.

The compelling compositions of amateur photographer and stationer Robert Louis Bracklow (1849-1919) document many sites, chiefly in Manhattan, with an eye toward preserving images of structures about to be torn down (Figure 31) and new structures ready to reshape the city environment. Bracklow captured such subjects as the remnants of a rural Upper West Side (Figure 32), skyscrapers under construction, shanties, a temporary tintype gallery, outmoded public water pumps, toy sailboats near large ships in the harbor, and outdoor statues. The platinum prints in his handmade albums provide glimpses of Coney Island crowds (Introduction, Figure 6), newsboys

Figure 32. West End Avenue and 89th Street, New York City. Platinum print by Robert L. Bracklow, 1902. (Neg. no. 60883)

The shanties and woman in a vegetable garden form a striking contrast with the urban row houses in the background. New buildings began to fill the Upper West Side after the elevated railroad lines extended to this part of Manhattan in the 1880s.

hawking Spanish-American War bulletins, the 1899 Dewey celebration (Figure 33), and excursions with friends to Long Island, Staten Island, New Jersey, Harper's Ferry, and New England. Bracklow (Introduction, Figure 11) was an active member of the Society of Amateur Photographers of New York (later the Camera Club), where he exhibited photographs with fellow amateur Richard H. Lawrence and with Alfred Stieglitz. Scenes with club members reflect the convivial atmosphere of photographic outings.

Arrangement and access: Most of the prints made by Bracklow are in albums and are described in one of his logbooks. His unmounted, often uncaptioned prints are grouped in folders by geographic area. The contact prints and enlargements made by Alexander Alland, ca. 1950, are filed by the numbers Alland assigned to the corresponding negatives. An unindexed 33-page finding aid lists the Alland contact prints and enlargements in numerical order. Bracklow's second logbook lists his negatives, but Alland's numbering system does not follow the same sequence. As a result, few of the prints made by Bracklow himself have been matched to an original negative. Many prints have copy negatives, which are indexed by subject in the Negative File catalog.
Provenance: Albums, vintage prints, and logbooks were donated by Ruth Trappan in 1983-1984. Modern contact prints and enlargements were purchased from Alexander Alland, ca. 1950. The negatives were a combined gift and purchase from Alland in 1983.
References: *Shanties to Skyscrapers: Robert L. Bracklow's Photographs of Early New York* (The New-York Historical Society exhibition catalog, 1983).

Figure 33. Sculpture by Daniel Chester French at base of the Dewey Arch, looking south along Fifth Avenue at Madison Square, New York City. Platinum print by Robert L. Bracklow, 1899. (Neg. no. 65015)

In 1899, New York City celebrated Admiral George Dewey's recent victory in the Spanish-American War with parades, naval maneuvers, and a full-scale plaster and wood model for a triumphal arch and colonnade. Too few subscriptions were received to build the actual monument, and the model was taken down in 1900.

Figure 34. *Buy My Apples*. Gelatin silver print by Browning, ca. 1930. (Neg. no. 58522)

Millions of people lost their jobs during the Great Depression. The man selling fruit in this photograph, taken in Manhattan, New York, has signs that say: "Help unemployed. Buy tangerines, 2 for 5 cents" and "Buy apples, 5 cents each."

9. BROWNING PHOTOGRAPH COLLECTION
1920s–1930s.
ca. 1,885 photographic prints (most 8 × 10 in.); a few film negatives.

Irving Browning (1895–1961), a self-taught photographer and cinematographer, opened a commercial photograph studio in New York City in the early 1920s. Skilled in appealing portrayal of new buildings, Irving and his younger brother Sam photographed exteriors and interiors of art deco theaters, hotels, apartment buildings, and suburban residences. Construction progress views document such skyscrapers as the Chrysler and Daily News buildings. The Brownings also captured close-ups of Manhattan shoppers and window displays, Lower East Side peddlers, advertising sandwich boards, roof tops, Great Depression shanty towns and street life (Figure 34), dramatic skylines (Figure 35), night views (Introduction, Figure 3), weather, sports, and many types of transportation. Samples of the photomontage technique Irving Browning developed for magazine clients complete the collection.

Arrangement and access: The briefly captioned photographs are filed by subject. A 17-page finding aid lists the 50 subject categories and indexes names of specific buildings, streets, and businesses.
Provenance: Gift from Irving Browning in 1959.
References: Wendy Shadwell, "The Browning Collection at The New-York Historical Society," *American Society of Picture Professionals Newsletter* 14 (Winter 1983): 1-3.
Related: Numerous Irving Browning professional association membership cards and exhibition notices are in the Landauer Collection.

Figure 35. View from a rooftop, looking northwest from Second Avenue and 39th Street toward Fifth Avenue and 42nd Streets, New York City. Photograph by Browning, 1930. (Neg. no. 57909)

The skyline features an impressive group of skyscrapers in Manhattan. From the left: 10 E. 40th St., Lefcourt Colonial Building, Lincoln Building, Chanin Building, Chrysler Building, and Daily News Building. Ironically, most of these ambitious construction projects of the 1920s were being completed in 1929–1930 just as the Great Depression started.

MOSE, LIZE, & LITTLE MOSE GOING TO CALIFORNIA.

By the overland Route, thus avoiding the Dangerous Chag-r-ass and Isth-m-ass passage and Depending entirely upon their Jackass.

Figure 36. *Mose, Lize & Little Mose Going to California.*
Lithograph by J.L. Magee, New York, 1849. (Neg. no. 21239)

When gold rush fever struck in 1849, New York City cartoonists responded with several comic prints about the lengths people would go to reach California. Artist John L. Magee portrayed a New York character (a Bowery B'hoy called Mose) racing past Catherine Market in a hastily loaded wagon.

10. CARICATURE AND CARTOON FILE
1750–present, bulk 1770–1910.
ca. 1,000 prints, most of which are engravings and lithographs; and ca. 1,000 pen and ink drawings.

Caustic and humorous pictorial commentary on political events and social customs blossomed in the mid-1700s with the publication of single-sheet caricatures. Such individually issued prints constitute the bulk of the Society's holdings, which also include drawings for editorial cartoons published in newspapers. Almost 600 prints date from before the Civil War, including British caricatures favoring United States independence and numerous protests of Andrew Jackson's policies. The California gold rush is lampooned in several cartoons issued in New York City (Figure 36) and in hand-colored lithographs in the rare portfolio *Album Californiano: Coleccion de Tipos Observados y Dibujados por los Sres. Ferran y Baturone* (Havana, ca. 1849–1850). Presidential elections, civil service reform, and tariffs are other popular topics. Major artists and publishers of lithographed cartoons are well-represented, including James Baillie, Edward W. Clay, Currier & Ives, David Claypoole Johnston, Henry R. Robinson, and Thomas W. Strong. Among the original pen and ink drawings are 35 by Thomas Nast, the chief American cartoonist of the 1870s and 1880s. There are also 903 drawings, ca. 1895–1912, by Homer C. Davenport, who was the leading editorial newspaper cartoonist of his day. Many of his images portray the seamier side of New York City politics or support Theodore Roosevelt. The world of newspaper comic strips is represented by some 50 original drawings, 1935–1936, donated by King Features Syndicate.

Arrangement and access: Prints and drawings are filed by date of execution. A card index, arranged by date, provides a brief description of each item, with cross references for titles and social satires. It includes caricatures in the Olds and Hyde collections. Access by artist is limited to works by Nast. The original drawings by Davenport are grouped by subject, and a checklist of topics serves as the finding aid. A reference file of 300 photographs reproduces most of the early cartoons.
References: Prints acquired before 1953 are cited in Frank Weitenkampf, *Political Caricature in the United States in Separately Published Cartoons: An Annotated List* (New York: New York Public Library, 1953).
Related: Non-political portrait caricatures are in the Portrait File. Photographic caricatures can be found in the Carte de Visite and Album files. The Joseph Keppler Collection is described in a separate guide entry. The Landauer Collection includes Yellow Kid material. The Peters Collection has cartoons from illustrated newspapers in its "Art" category. A few cartoon drawings by John N. Bulkley and by Alan Dunn are in the Department of Paintings, Sculpture, and Decorative Arts. Published magazine and newspaper cartoons can be found in the Reading Room's extensive periodical collection.

Figure 37. Henry Jarvis Raymond (1820-1869), founding editor of *The New York Times*. Carte de visite published by E. & H.T. Anthony, from photographic negative by Brady, ca. 1865. (Neg. no. 1202)

11. CARTE DE VISITE PHOTOGRAPH FILE

ca. 1860-1900, bulk 1860s.
ca. 6,100 photographic prints, most albumen on card mounts (2½ × 4 in.); some engravings, lithographs, and photo-mechanical prints on card mounts of the same size.

The carte de visite photograph was patented in France in 1854 and became the chief commercial portrait medium in the 1860s. These inexpensive prints, mounted on card stock the size of a calling card, remained available into the 1900s. The majority of images in the Society's file date from the 1860s and show only the person's head and shoulders. Many depict soldiers and officers in Civil War uniform. Later cards feature full-length figures posed in studio settings (Figure 37). Of special interest are composite caricatures by Charles D. Fredericks in which a photographic head is combined with a cartoon body drawing. New York City scenes, Civil War views (including ca. 50 from Mathew Brady's *Album Gallery*) (Figure 38), and copies of miscellaneous paintings and objects complete the file. Anyone seeking nationally or locally prominent persons (Figure 39), international celebrities, or Union Army soldiers should consult the file. Researchers with time to examine numerous cards will find material of interest for costume history and photographic history. A spot check of imprints reveals work from such leading carte de visite producers as: E. & H.T. Anthony, D. Appleton & Co., Mathew Brady, Jeremiah Gurney & Son, José M. Mora, George G. Rockwood, and Napoleon Sarony.

Arrangement and access: Cartes de visite are filed alphabetically by the name of the sitter, with separate small categories for African Americans; Indians; Circus; Theatrical; Groups; Unidentified Men, Women, and Children; Civil War; City Views; Caricatures; and Miscellaneous. There is no index by photographer.
Related: Many cartes de visite are in albums in the Album File and can be located through the Album File card index. Most carte de visite theatrical portraits and city views have been mounted on larger sheets and can be found throughout the Portrait File and Geographic File. The Landauer Collection scrapbook for photography includes more than 150 cartes de visite.

Figure 38. *Confederate Graves, Centreville.* Carte de visite copyrighted by Barnard & Gibson, 1862. *Brady's Album Gallery,* no. 304. (Neg. no. 65018)

While working for Mathew Brady, photographers George Barnard and John Gibson took this view in the Bull Run battle vicinity in Virginia. Printed on the back of the card is a quotation: "Did these bones cost no more the breeding, but to play at loggats with them. Mine ache to think on't." An additional note says: "The photographs of this series were taken directly from nature, at considerable cost. Warning is therefore given that legal proceedings will be at once instituted against any party infringing the copyright."

Figure 39. *Sojourner Truth. I Sell the Shadow to Support the Substance.* Carte de visite by unidentified photographer, copyrighted by Truth in 1864. (Neg. no. 47465)

Sojourner Truth (1797–1883) was born into slavery in Ulster County, New York. In the 1840s, she began to preach and travel and became a well-known advocate for abolition and later for women's suffrage. She also used the carte de visite craze to good advantage. Starting in 1863, she raised some of her income by selling photographic portraits of herself.

Figure 40. *Caesar, a slave.* Daguerreotype by unidentified photographer, 1851. (Neg. no. 46594)

Caesar (died 1852) was born on the Nicoll family estate on the Hudson River near Albany, New York. Although New York state law freed the slaves within its borders by 1827, Caesar remained with the Nicolls through six generations.

12. CASED PHOTOGRAPH FILE

ca. 1850–1900, bulk 1850–1870.
Ca. 1,600 photographs; most are daguerreotypes and ambrotypes; many are tintypes;
a few are opalotypes and other small photographs on glass or enamel (usually ca. 4 × 5 in. or smaller).
Accompanied by empty cases with decorated covers.

Portraits constitute most of the file, in keeping with the predominant subject matter of daguerreotypes (1840s–1850s) and ambrotypes (1850s–1860s). Most are still in the miniature cases in which they were sold. The file also contains such uncased non-paper formats as tintypes, opalotypes, and other small photographs on glass or enamel that require special handling. Heavily represented family groups include the Beekman, Peter Cooper, de Groot, Delano, Abram S. Hewitt, John Rogers, Schermerhorn, Schuyler, and Emma Thursby families and associates. Such prominent Americans as Henry Clay, Asher B. Durand, Millard Fillmore, Washington Irving, Jenny Lind, John McComb, William H. Seward, and Daniel Webster appear in sharp detail in the mirror-surface of daguerreotypes. Other striking images include Caesar, a New York slave (Figure 40); the 1856 Rutgers Female Institute graduating class; and an unidentified mother and child in a stereograph daguerreotype viewer patented by J.F. Mascher of Philadelphia. Among the few views are an interior of the New York Crystal Palace in the 1850s (Introduction, Figure 13) and a Niagara Falls landscape. Most of the photographers operated in New York City, for example: Rufus Anson, Abraham Bogardus, Mathew Brady, Charles D. Fredericks, Jeremiah Gurney, Silas A. Holmes, and John Plumbe.

Arrangement and access: The largest section is alphabetical by sitter. The smaller sections are Unidentified Sitter by Identified Photographer (filed by photographer); Unidentified Sitter by Unidentified Photographer; Subjects (e.g., Niagara Falls); and Empty Cases. A card index describes each image in detail. Unusual types (e.g., post-mortem portraits) are cross-referenced under the category called "Special." Photographer's name, medium, date, and case design are also indexed. A visual finding aid (a copy of each image on 35mm contact sheets) provides initial access to the photographs and makes it possible to search for such unindexed characteristics as portraits with dolls.

Related: Tintypes may also be found in the Album, Portrait, and Stereograph files. The Photographer Reference Index provides brief biographical data for some 30 New York State daguerreotypists and ambrotypists. Many of the family portrait groups are associated with family papers in the Manuscript Department. The Department of Paintings, Sculpture, and Decorative Arts has some examples of jewelry that incorporate photographs.

13. CATHEDRAL CHURCH OF ST. JOHN THE DIVINE PHOTOGRAPH COLLECTION

ca. 1895–1940, bulk 1900–1930.
ca. 1,050 photographic prints (most platinum and palladiotype) and ca. 2,700 glass negatives (most 5 × 7 in., also 4 × 5 in., 8 × 10 in., and 11 × 14 in.). Accompanied by photogravure illustrations for *The Word in Stone*.

The Protestant Episcopal Cathedral Church of St. John the Divine, one of the world's largest cathedrals, has been under construction since 1892. Antoinette Bryant Hervey (1857–1945) lived near the cathedral on Morningside Heights in upper Manhattan and avidly recorded developments from every angle (Figures 41 and 42). She became known as photographer to a cathedral and reproduced several of her finest images in *The Word in Stone* to help raise building funds. Most of Hervey's images at the Society are in a pictorial style developed during her days as a student at the Clarence H. White School of Photography, beginning in 1914. Hervey's artistic documentation ranges from details of the baptistery roof vault and sculpture faces to general chapel interiors and snowy exteriors. Her widespread photographic society activities are reflected in the many exhibition stickers still on the larger matted views. The balance of the collection is 600 negatives taken by other photographers for Bishop Henry C. Potter, between ca. 1895 and 1910, and 300 prints made by Hervey in 1939 from those negatives.

Arrangement and access: Prints are filed by size (8 × 10 in. or smaller, and larger than 8 × 10 in.), then by date or part of the cathedral. Negatives are stored by size and then date, with undated images at the end of the sequence. The finding aid is a checklist of prints and negatives arranged by filing categories. The relationship between prints and negatives is not easily determined, because prints have not been made for all negatives and negative numbers are only on some of the prints.
Provenance: Gift from Antoinette B. Hervey in 1940.
References: Walter L. Hervey, *Memories and Records of Antoinette Bryant Hervey* (Privately published, 1946).
At other institutions: The Library of Congress, Prints and Photographs Division has ca. 50 signed and dated prints by Hervey of the Cathedral.

Figure 41. *The Cathedral from My Window at 351 West 114th Street.* Platinum print by Antoinette B. Hervey, March 1928. (Neg. no. 70810)

Figure 42. Altar and columns, Cathedral Church of St. John the Divine, New York City. Platinum print by Antoinette B. Hervey, December 1921. (Neg. no. 70809)

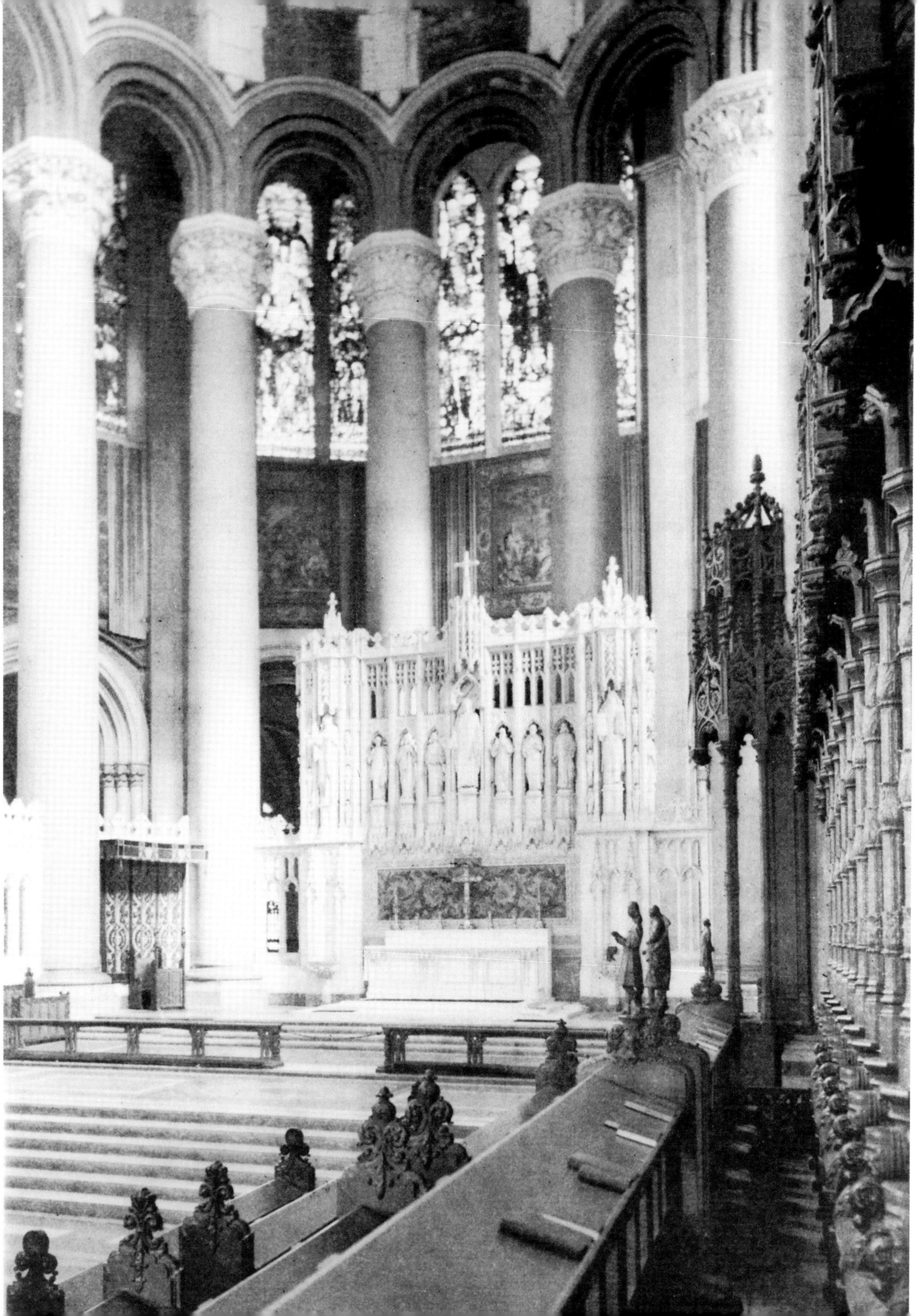

14. CERTIFICATE FILE

ca. 1750–present, bulk 1790–1900.
ca. 600 prints, including engravings, lithographs, and photomechanical prints; some hand-drawn.

Although most certificates are issued in multiple copies, the relatively few that survive often document little known organizations or aid the study of early American printing. The Society's file consists chiefly of illustrated certificates and printing specimens. One of the earliest, a British testimonial for Indian allies, depicts Sir William Johnson presenting a medal to an Iroquois chief. (This impression, probably printed ca. 1820, was donated with the original copperplate engraved by Henry Dawkins in 1770.) Also of special interest are the maritime relief association memberships, firemen appointments (Figure 43), rewards of merit, temperance pledges, and subscriptions to build monuments. The most numerous certificates are for memberships in political, social, fraternal, agricultural, philanthropic, and religious societies; college and school documents; and military papers. There are also a few coats of arms, passports, marriage and baptismal certificates, and stock certificates.

Arrangement and access: The file has more than 10 categories based on the type of issuing organization or certificate. For most categories, a card index lists the names of the organizations that issued the certificates. A catalog describing each item has been started, with indexes by certificate issuer, certificate owner, date, and artist or printmaker.

Related: The Landauer Collection includes many certificates interfiled with other ephemera. Fraktur certificates are in the Graphic Arts File. Certificates are also in the Manuscript Department, usually as part of family or business papers.

Figure 43. Firemen of the City of New York certificate for John Meyers, dated Dec. 23, 1791. Engraving attributed to Abraham Godwin, ca. 1791. (Neg. no. 48533)

An action-filled fire scene and fire equipment decorate the borders of this certificate. New York City relied on volunteer firefighters such as John Meyers until 1865.

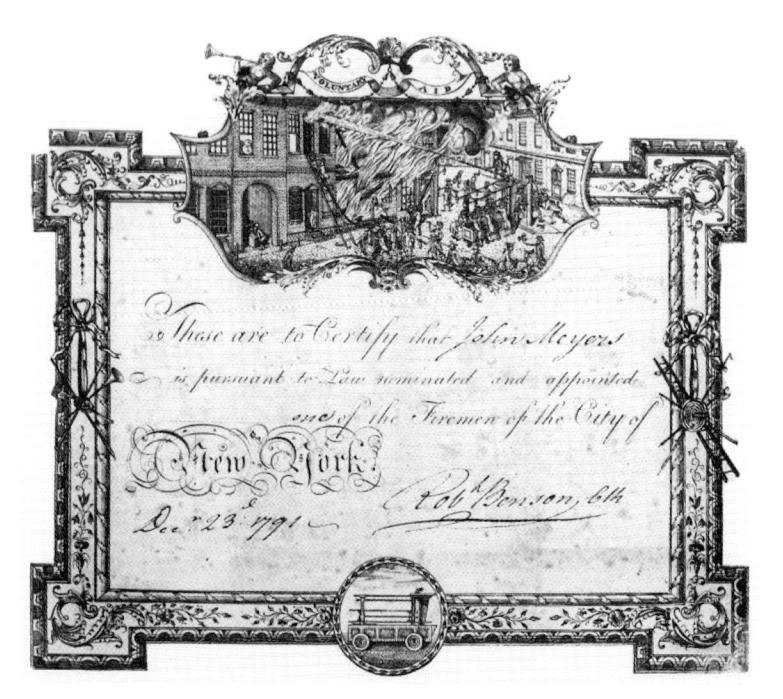

Figure 44. *Diagonals.* Gelatin silver print by Arthur D. Chapman, 1914. (Neg. no. 66765)

In the 1918 *American Annual of Photography*, Chapman wrote that pictures "made within ten minutes' walk of my own hypo-tank are the most interesting to me… because I have discovered for myself that pictures can be 'seen' anywhere, if only the artist will forget that he is looking at familiar things. This is not easy.… I used one of the Sixth Avenue elevated stations twice a day for several months and then found 'Diagonals.' This print has been shown in more photographic exhibitions than any other I have made." The view is looking down Christopher Street from the elevated railroad platform in Manhattan.

15. ARTHUR D. CHAPMAN PHOTOGRAPH COLLECTION
1908–1922 and 1953, bulk 1910s.
58 photographic prints (most 6 × 8 in. or 8 × 10 in. on mounts 18 × 14 in.).

Amateur photographer Arthur D. Chapman (1882–1956) worked nights as a newspaper printer and in the afternoons turned his view camera on New York City's outdoor shapes. He took special pride in discovering compositions of pictorial interest in his everyday surroundings, and his best-known images portray non-Bohemian Greenwich Village in the 1910s. The Society's collection includes skyscrapers looming at the end of narrow streets, snow-covered parks and rooflines (Figure 44), bridges, boat basins, and construction sites. Greenwich Village appears in almost 20 soft-focus scenes featuring such details as laundry lines and an unattended baby carriage on Milligan Place. Two self-portraits with photographic equipment, dated 1913 and 1953, indicate an enduring interest in photography. Each image has a short title and is signed and dated.

Arrangement and access: Prints are filed by acquisition date. A card in the Photographer Reference Index briefly describes the photographs.
Provenance: Purchase and gift from the photographer in 1950–1955.

Figure 45. Grace Hill for Edwin C. Litchfield, Brooklyn, New York. Watercolor by Alexander J. Davis, ca. 1855. (Neg. no. 55257)

Davis designed this Italianate-style villa for Edwin Clark Litchfield (1815–1885), a successful railroad and real estate investor, and his family. The drawing of the front elevation and principal floor plan shows a tower porch, hall, dining room, drawing room, parlor, library, bedroom, dressing room, bathroom, pantry, and lift. The house still stands in Brooklyn's Prospect Park and is called Litchfield Villa.

16. ALEXANDER J. DAVIS ARCHITECTURAL DRAWING COLLECTION

ca. 1830–ca. 1880.
ca. 800 architectural drawings, chiefly renderings and plans in ink, graphite, and watercolor.
Accompanied by *Rural Residences*.

The innovative and influential architect Alexander Jackson Davis (1803–1892) designed many buildings between 1830 and 1860, the peak years of his long career. Davis studied to be an artist, and many of his skillful architectural illustrations appeared in the *New-York Mirror* and in books by Andrew Jackson Downing. An 1829–1835 partnership with established New York architect Ithiel Town brought Davis to prominence as they collaborated on such Greek Revival monuments as the Indiana State Capitol. Davis is best known for his romantic country villas and cottages, which are represented in this collection by some 200 drawings and by his 1838 publication *Rural Residences*. The picturesque Gothic Revival, Italianate, and bracketed-style residences were built mostly in the Hudson River area, but clients came from as far north as Maine and as far south as North Carolina. Many houses appear in only a single sheet, although a set of 23 drawings covers Litchfield Villa in Brooklyn (Figure 45), one of his few surviving New York City structures. The remaining drawings depict more than 150 different projects designed or sketched by Davis: numerous churches and public buildings, including the Brooklyn City Hall; several office and commercial buildings; art galleries, schools, historical societies, and libraries, including an unexecuted scheme for the Astor Library; asylums and hospitals; and monuments. Only some of the drawings are fully identified and dated; most are signed. Compared with other collections of Davis' works, the Society's collection is particularly strong in New York City and State material.

Arrangement and access: Drawings are filed by Society-assigned numbers. A card catalog indexes building type and style and provides information about project or client name, date, and number of drawings.
Provenance: Samuel V. Hoffmann presented 675 drawings in 1927. Edward S. Litchfield donated some of the Litchfield Mansion designs in 1976. Additional drawings were received from other sources.
References: About 20 of the drawings are illustrated in Amelia Peck, editor, *Alexander Jackson Davis, American Architect, 1803–1892* (New York: Metropolitan Museum of Art and Rizzoli, 1992), with an introduction by Jane B. Davies. About 200 of the drawings are described in George S. Koyl, editor, *American Architectural Drawings: A Catalog …* (Philadelphia: Philadelphia Chapter, American Institute of Architects, 1969).
Related: Lithographs by Anthony Imbert from drawings by Davis are in the Printmaker File. An album of drawings presented to Davis by John Trumbull is in the Architect and Engineer File. The Manuscript Department has a list of Davis' architectural books, ca. 10 drawings, and some correspondence. The Department of Paintings, Sculpture, and Decorative Arts has ca. 30 drawings by Davis, most for illustrations in the *New-York Mirror* in the 1820s.
At other institutions: Other large collections of Davis material are at the Avery Architectural and Fine Arts Library at Columbia University, the Metropolitan Museum of Art, and the New York Public Library.

17. LESLIE DORSEY COLLECTION OF PICTORIAL CLIPPINGS

ca. 1860s–1970s, bulk 1860–1920.
ca. 150 scrapbooks, with wood engravings and other book and magazine illustrations; newspaper articles; also, some ephemera and photographic prints.

Leslie Dorsey (died 1979) designed hotel interiors and became interested in hotel history. With Janice Devine, he wrote *Fare Thee Well: A Backward Look at Two Centuries of Historic American Hostelries, Fashionable Spas & Seaside Resorts* (New York: Crown Publishers, 1964). Dorsey also pursued his fascination with the past, especially Victorian and Edwardian era public entertainments, by filling scrapbooks with vintage magazine and book illustrations and some original greeting cards, programs, and other ephemera. The largest segment of the collection includes such categories as Edwardian theater; expositions (Crystal Palace, Centennial, Columbian, Louisiana Purchase, and Pan-American); dining, drinking, and hotels; Christmas; and sports. The New York City segment contains 11 volumes, most of which provide a few views of many topics. Two volumes cover hotels, and one book is a well-captioned pictorial history of 23rd Street in Manhattan. Other binders contain wood engravings advertising such products as bricks, brushes, and butter. There are also fashion prints (arranged chronologically); material related to the new Metropolitan Opera, the United States Bicentennial, and Colorado hotels; and newspaper articles on New York City history.

Arrangement and access: The scrapbooks are grouped in broad categories: New York City Illustrations, General Illustrations, Wood Engravings, Fashion, New York City History Articles, New Metropolitan Opera, U.S. Bicentennial, and Colorado. The finding aid is a checklist of scrapbook topics, for some of which photocopies are available for ready reference. There is also an alphabetical card index to major subjects. More detailed indexes, compiled by Dorsey, accompany several categories, including New York City and General Illustrations.
Provenance: Bequest from Leslie Dorsey in 1979.

18. FIFTH AVENUE COACH COMPANY PHOTOGRAPH COLLECTION

ca. 1890–1955, bulk 1910s–1920s.
ca. 800 mounted photographs (7 × 9 in.) and 2 scrapbooks with photographs, ephemera, and clippings.

The Fifth Avenue Coach Company operated buses in Manhattan from 1885 until the 1950s, most memorably the double-decker type. The company compiled this series of public relation photographs to show off its fine customer and employee facilities, which included a staff barber shop, reading room, and pool table for off-duty hours. The instructional views of the right and wrong ways to operate a bus are often comical, but along with the scenes of bus construction and World War I public service projects (Figure 46), they evidence the company's pride in its efficiency and courtesy. Other parts of the archive chronicle developments in bus design from wood-panel to steel construction. There are also scrapbooks with brochures for special excursions and regular routes.

Arrangement and access: Mounted prints are filed in a chronological sequence established by the company. A set of photocopies is available for reference.
Provenance: Gift from the Metropolitan Transportation Authority in 1981.

Figure 46. *2A-Type Bus Camouflaged—Woman's Motor Corps of America.*
Photograph by unidentified photographer, ca. 1917. (Neg. no. 58504)

Two women are painting a dollar sign on a double-decker bus
to sell Liberty bonds in New York City to raise funds during World War I.

Figure 47. *Friends.* Photograph by Arnold Genthe, ca. 1915. (Neg. no. 64185)

Genthe's cat Buzzer is lying in a chair with a doll. In his autobiography *As I Remember*, Genthe wrote: "Just as my love for horses dates back to my early childhood, so does my affection for cats. Their sheer physical beauty and consummate grace as well as the air of inscrutable mystery have always had a strong appeal for me. I prefer cats that have a deep purr and for that reason every cat I have owned was called 'Buzzer.'"

19. ARNOLD GENTHE PHOTOGRAPH COLLECTION
ca. 1900-1942.
70 photographic prints (some color) and several photomechanical halftone prints; ca. 3,000 film negatives and a few glass transparencies (most 4 × 5 in. and smaller, some 5 × 7 in.).

Master photographer Arnold Genthe (1869-1942) emigrated in 1895 from his native Germany to San Francisco, where he taught himself photography and gained recognition for views of Chinatown street life and portraits of people prominent in art and society circles. He moved his studio to Manhattan in 1911. The Society's holdings represent most of Genthe's interests: pictorial portraiture, classical beauty in dance and in architectural studies, picturesque documentary views, and color photography. The vintage prints, few of which are signed or dated, depict such people as authors Jack London and Edna St. Vincent Millay (Introduction, Figure 14), actress Mary Pickford, and artists Childe Hassam and James Montgomery Flagg. Chinatown scenes, dance studies, and color views and portraits complete the print section. Subjects depicted in the negatives (and identified on the original negative jackets) include famous personalities, among them Greta Garbo and J.P. Morgan; Genthe on horseback; numerous sitters for routine portraits; Chinatown; New York City buildings in 1931; Long Island houses, gardens, and hunting; Westchester (New York) Country Club; White Sulphur Springs, West Virginia; New Orleans; Salt Lake City; European travel; Guatemala; Japan; dance groups; and cats (Figure 47). Dated negatives span 1913-1942, but the size of the Chinatown film negatives suggests that they may be the original 1890s exposures from his handheld camera.

Arrangement and access: Prints are grouped in broad categories—Portraits, Chinatown, Dance, and Miscellaneous. The finding aid is a checklist of print titles within each category and a summary of subjects depicted in the negatives.
Provenance: The Society purchased the prints at Genthe's estate auction in 1943. The negatives were donated in 1954 and 1957 by the Library of Congress, which distributed variant view photographs to several institutions.
At other institutions: The bulk of the photographs in Genthe's studio at his death are now at the Library of Congress, Prints and Photographs Division. Several thousand negatives are also at the Museum of the City of New York. Many museums and libraries have prints by Genthe.

20. GEOGRAPHIC FILE

ca. 1500–present, bulk 1850–1950.

ca. 45,000 thousand prints and photographs.

The Geographic File contains both topographical views and images of local events. Approximately half of the file covers New York City, especially Manhattan. Several sets of prints, for example, those published in the 1830s by George M. Bourne and by Peabody & Co., portray a prosperous metropolis of elegant buildings and thriving commerce. Several thousand carefully captioned street views feature groups of buildings, commercial signs, and vehicles (Introduction, Figures 4 and 12). They complement images of individual bridges, businesses, churches, clubs, hospitals, hotels, and restaurants (including photographs from the W. Johnson Quinn Collection), libraries and museums, parks, residences (Figure 48), and theaters. There are also prints and photographs of the harbor, parades, civic celebrations, fires, the memorable blizzards of 1888 and 1947, and election campaigns. Numerous photographs feature transportation by street railroads and by elevated railroads. Among the more unusual items is a group of European peep show prints, called vues d'optique, which were published in the 1770s and portray New York fictitiously as a European citadel. Professional photographers and printmakers created most of the images. Those represented by numerous works include John Bachmann, John H. Bufford, Currier & Ives, Endicott & Co., John S. Johnston, Beecher Ogden, Wiliam J. Roege, Sarony & Major, and Herman N. Tiemann. Amateur photographers have contributed special projects, such as Ernest L. Scott's record of the George Washington Bridge construction, 1929–1931 (Introduction, Figures 7 and 8). Other concentrations of material include images of the Bronx gathered by Edmund B. Child and subway material preserved by Arthur Weindorf. Some men provided images related to books they wrote: William F. Reeves gathered many rare early photographs of elevated railroads; Hopper Striker Mott documented the Bloomingdale area; and Alvin F. Harlow focused on the Bowery.

The second half of the file covers the rest of New York State, other U.S. states, and several foreign countries. The most noteworthy cityscapes and landscapes include pre-Civil War views of major United States cities. For example, a rare lithograph by Anthony Fleetwood printed in New York in 1834 is the earliest known view of Detroit. There are also many lithographs by Edwin Whitefield, engravings of Niagara Falls and West Point, and early photographs of San Francisco. Bird's-eye view panoramic maps document many upstate New York communities from ca. 1870 to 1900 (Figure 49). Souvenir viewbooks summarize city highlights from ca. 1890 to 1910. Hundreds of photographs by Eugene L. Armbruster, George W. Nash, and John J. Vrooman record historic structures, chiefly on Long Island and in the Hudson River Valley.

Figure 48. Double parlor, M.M. Van Beuren residence, 21 West 14th Street, New York City. Photograph by Pach Brothers, N.Y., ca. 1875. (Neg. no. 25904)

The parlor includes a piano and a suite of furniture by Charles Baudouine.

Arrangement and access: Prints and photographs are filed by country, state, and city, with subdivisions in extensively represented cities for building types, street names, parades, and other subjects. The New York City material has a finding aid checklist of filing categories. Many items have been photographed and are indexed in the Negative File catalog, which provides some access by photographer or printmaker as well as by place name.
References: Many of the Manhattan prints are noted in I.N. Phelps Stokes, *The Iconography of Manhattan Island, 1498-1909,* 6 vols. (New York: R.H. Dodd, 1915-1928). Almost 200 New York City photographs are illustrated in Mary Black, *Old New York in Early Photographs, 1853-1901,* 2d rev. ed. (New York: Dover, 1976). Bird's-eye view prints are recorded in John W. Reps, *Views and Viewmakers of Urban America:... A Union Catalog of Their Work, 1825-1925* (Columbia: University of Missouri Press, 1984).
Related: The Postcard and Stereograph files contain many geographic scenes. Topographic views in other collections can be located under place names in the index to this guide. The Manuscript Department has several hundred city views in extra-illustrated sets of *Old New York* by John Francis. The Reading Room has numerous illustrated local history publications. The Department of Paintings, Sculpture, and Decorative Arts also has many cityscapes and landscapes.
At other institutions: Strong collections of New York views are at the Museum of the City of New York, the New York Public Library, and the New York State Historical Association.

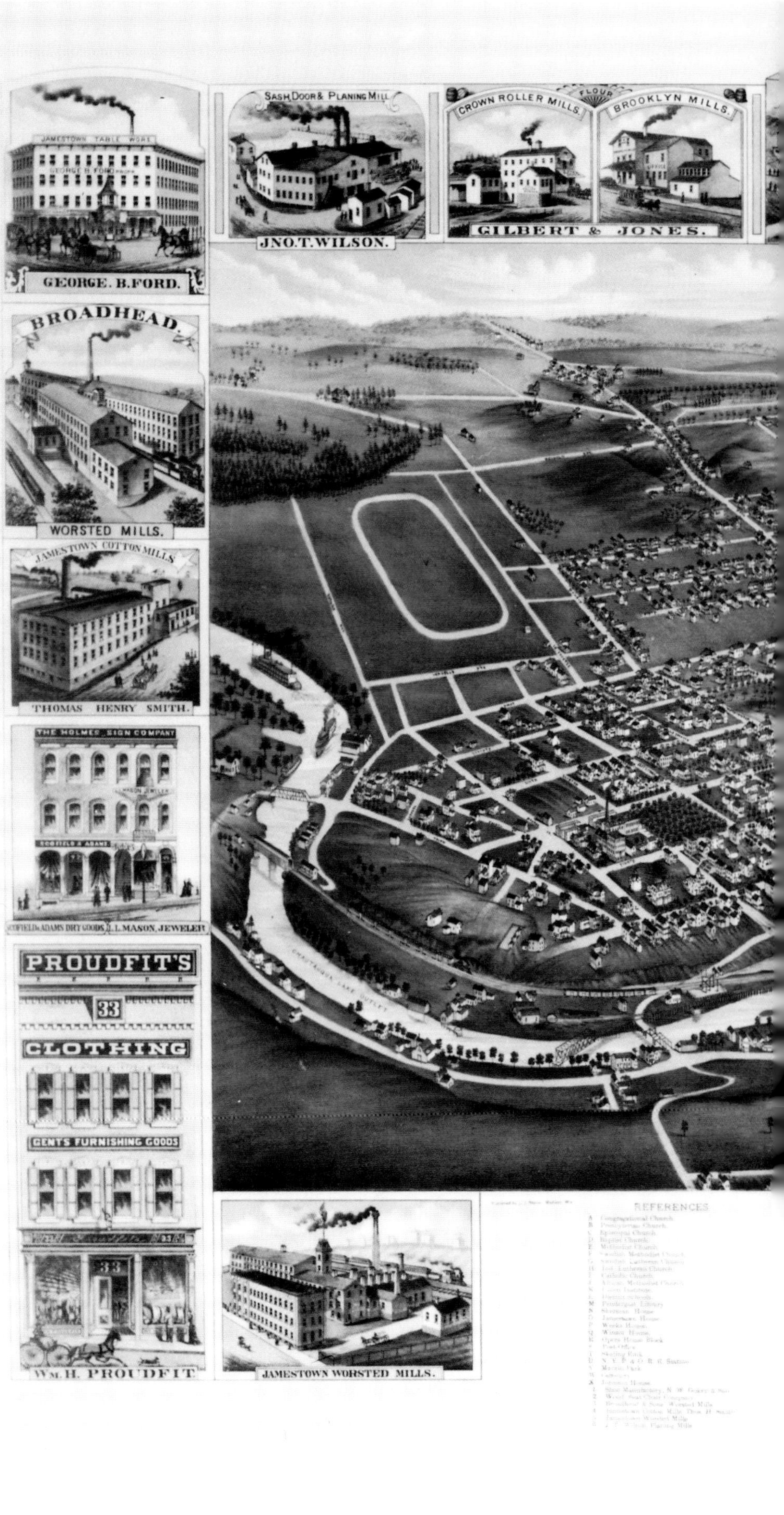

Figure 49. *Bird's Eye View of the Village of Jamestown, Chautauqua County, New York, Looking North East.* Drawn by H. Brosius and A.F. Poole. Color lithograph printed by Beck & Pauli, Milwaukee, Wisconsin, and published and copyrighted by J.J. Stoner, Madison, Wisconsin, 1882. (Neg. no. 53552)

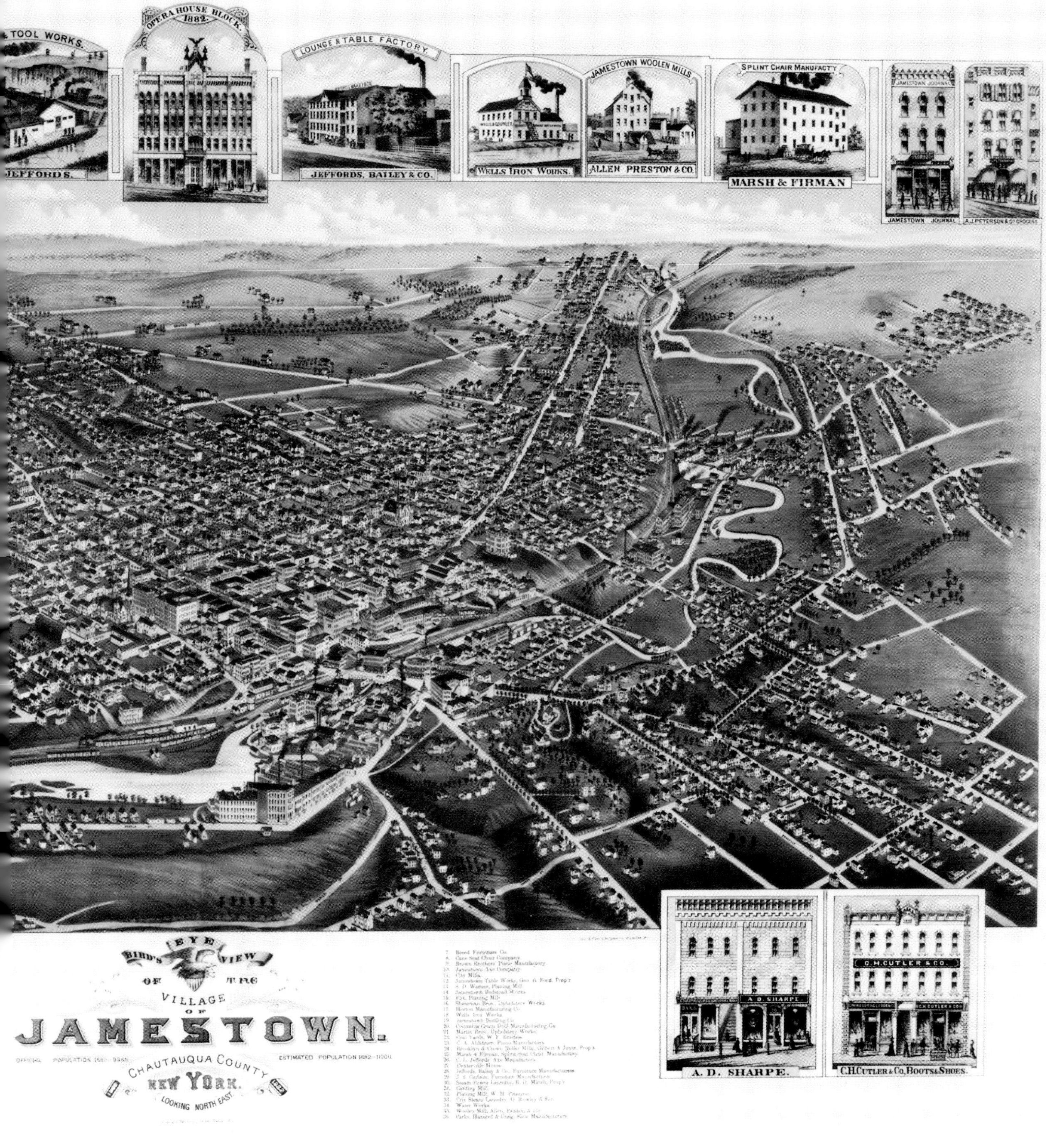

TOOL WORKS.
JEFFORDS.
OPERA HOUSE BLOCK. 1882.
LOUNGE & TABLE FACTORY.
JEFFORDS, BAILEY & CO.
WELLS IRON WORKS.
JAMESTOWN WOOLEN MILLS.
ALLEN PRESTON & CO.
SPLINT CHAIR MANUFACT'Y
MARSH & FIRMAN
JAMESTOWN JOURNAL
JAMESTOWN JOURNAL
A.J. PETERSON & CO. GROCERS
A. D. SHARPE
A. D. SHARPE.
C.H. CUTLER & CO.
C.H. CUTLER & CO. BOOTS & SHOES.
BIRD'S EYE VIEW OF THE VILLAGE OF JAMESTOWN.
OFFICIAL POPULATION 1880–9365
ESTIMATED POPULATION 1882–11000
CHAUTAUQUA COUNTY NEW YORK.
LOOKING NORTH EAST.
1882
7. Breed Furniture Co.
8. Cane Seat Chair Company
9. Brown Brothers' Piano Manufactory
10. Jamestown Axe Company
11. City Mills
12. Jamestown Table Works, Geo. B. Ford, Prop'r
13. S. D. Warner, Planing Mill
14. Jamestown Bedstead Works
15. Fox, Planing Mill
16. Shearman Bros., Upholstery Works
17. Horton Manufacturing Co.
18. Wells Iron Works
19. Jamestown Bedding Co.
20. Columbus Grain Drill Manufacturing Co.
21. Martin Bros., Upholstery Works
22. Coal Yards, W. F. Endress
23. C. A. Ahlstrom, Piano Manufactory
24. Brooklyn & Crown Roller Mills, Gilbert & Jones, Prop's
25. Marsh & Firman, Splint Seat Chair Manufactory
26. C. L. Jeffords' Axe Manufactory
27. Dexterville House
28. Jeffords, Bailey & Co., Furniture Manufacturers
29. J. S. Carlson, Furniture Manufacturer
30. Steam Power Laundry, B. H. Marsh, Prop'r
31. Carding Mill
32. Planing Mill, W. H. Peterson
33. City Steam Laundry, D. Rowley & Son
34. Water Works
35. Woolen Mill, Allen, Preston & Co.
36. Parks, Hazzard & Craig, Shoe Manufacturers

Figures 50-51. Woolworth Building (Broadway at Park Place, New York City), designed by Cass Gilbert. Left: Preliminary sketch by Cass Gilbert, ca. 1908, (Neg. no. 32066). Right: Study by Thomas R. Johnson, April 25, 1910. (Neg. no. 45872)

This pair of drawings illustrates how an architect develops and changes design ideas. In 1913, when the Woolworth Building opened, it was the tallest skyscraper in the world. Masonry and terra-cotta cover the steel frame of this Gothic-style office building, which is sometimes called a "cathedral of commerce."

21. CASS GILBERT ARCHITECTURAL RECORD COLLECTION

1879-1934.
ca. 63,000 architectural drawings, including blueprints, ink drawings on linen, and other media; 5,000 pencil sketches and watercolor renderings; 4 travel sketchbooks; 245 cubic feet of incoming correspondence; 469 volumes of outgoing correspondence; 75 volumes of specifications; ca. 11 cubic feet of photographs; 15 cash books, journals, and payroll ledgers (1899-1934); 6 clipping scrapbooks; 2 appointment diaries; 7 drawing ledgers.

Architect Cass Gilbert (1859-1934) studied for a year at the Massachusetts Institute of Technology and traveled in Europe before apprenticing with McKim, Mead & White in New York from 1880 to 1882. Gilbert then returned to St. Paul, Minnesota, and practiced in partnership with James

Knox Taylor until 1892, when he started his own firm. He established a New York office in 1898 and by the end of his long career had worked on some 600 projects documented in his corporate archive at the Society. A list of Gilbert's best-known structures indicates the national scope and large scale of his commissions: the Minnesota State Capitol; United States Custom House, New York; St. Louis Art Museum; West Street Building, New York; his masterpiece, the Woolworth Building, New York (Figures 50 and 51); New York Life Insurance Building, New York; and the United States Supreme Court, Washington, D.C. Gilbert also designed many private residences, churches, and commercial structures in the St. Paul, Minnesota, area. In New York City and neighboring areas of Connecticut and New Jersey, he undertook apartment buildings, banks, bridges, city halls, clubs, colleges, court houses, hospitals, hotels, libraries, museums, office buildings, railroad stations, schools, stores, tombs and memorials, and warehouses. His early work in Minnesota is usually characterized as picturesque and his later work as Beaux-Arts tradition, with the exception of the more Gothic style West Street and Woolworth buildings.

Examples of past queries indicate the range of research topics to which this large archive can contribute: structural engineering of skyscrapers; freestanding rotunda construction; paint specifications (for a building restoration); politics of architectural competitions; college campus plans; sculptural work by Daniel Chester French; renderings by Hugh Ferriss, Jules Guérin, Thomas R. Johnson, and others; the organizational and business side of a prosperous firm; client-architect and architect-contractor relationships; professional association interactions; and design development from initial proposal to completed building.

Arrangement and access: The Society began a major preservation and cataloging project in 1990. The finding aid is an alphabetical index listing names of buildings by Gilbert as well as individuals and organizations with which he corresponded. As the drawings are cataloged, information about designs and buildings will be available in a database.
Provenance: Gift from the architect's children, Cass Gilbert, Jr., and Emily Gilbert, in 1956 and 1957.
References: Sharon L. Irish, "Cass Gilbert's Career in New York, 1899-1905" (Ph.D. dissertation, Northwestern University, 1985.)
At other institutions: The Library of Congress, Prints and Photographs Division, has several hundred sketches by Cass Gilbert, and the Library of Congress, Manuscript Division, has thousands of his personal papers. The Avery Architectural and Fine Arts Library at Columbia University has miscellaneous drawings and papers. Material can also be found in other organizations—for example, in the archives of Gilbert's public institution clients and of the professional organizations to which he belonged.

22. GRAPHIC ARTS FILE
ca. 1500–present, bulk 1800–1900.
ca. 5,000 prints, chiefly engravings and lithographs.

The Graphic Arts File is an umbrella category for special ephemera formats, for material saved because of its association to a particular artist or art collection, and for miscellaneous specimens of American and European printing. The special format ephemera includes more than 100 clipper ship cards, chiefly examples printed in colors on enameled card stock by the New York City firm of George F. Nesbitt in the 1850s and 1860s. These prized examples of commercial printing were distributed to inform prospective passengers and freight shippers of the impending departure of such speedy vessels as the *Shooting Star* and *White Swallow* (Figure 52). There are also nearly 200 unused pictorial lettersheets from the 1840s to 1880s, many of which were published by Charles Magnus by transforming photographs of New York City into hand-colored lithographic scenes (Figure 53). An album of California gold rush lettersheets printed by Britton & Rey includes views of miners' quarters and a San Francisco hanging. The patriotic envelopes popular during the Civil War are represented in about 3,000 pro-Union and pro-Confederate examples, including several hundred by Magnus. Among the most charming ephemera are paper roses—circular sheets folded in a pie wedge shape, with a blooming rose decoration, which unfolds to reveal color vignettes of New York City landmarks printed ca. 1850.

The 1937 acquisition of the Elie Nadelman Folk Art Collection brought the Society examples of fraktur illuminations, including more than 30 birth and baptismal certificates, house blessings and spiritual texts printed in Pennsylvania as early as the 1780s. The bulk of the games also come from the Nadelman Collection. They feature several hundred American and European playing cards and educational decks from 1546 to 1900, several board games, paper dolls, and French pantins. Pictorial calendars comprise another large ephemera format category. The 500 examples date from the 1870s to 1950s, with the heaviest representation after 1940. Most were issued by banks or insurance companies and are illustrated with re-creations of key events in United States history or with Currier & Ives scenes.

Material saved because of its association with a New York art collector or artist includes ca. 160 European prints acquired with the Bryan Collection paintings in 1867. Thomas J. Bryan opened one of New York's first public art rooms, the Bryan Gallery of Christian Art, in order to bring European culture to the United States. Another indicator of American taste and interest in art can be found in the almost 90 European prints once owned by the New York Gallery of the Fine

Figure 52. *White Swallow* clipper ship card.
Color woodcut by Nesbitt & Co., N.Y., ca. 1862.
(Neg. no. 46620)

Arts and in the ca. 250 European prints from the Louis Durr Collection, which include religious scenes, reproductions of paintings, and portraits. There are also graphic materials associated with four artists active in the 1800s whose original drawings, paintings, or papers are owned by the Society: engravings and photomechanical reproductions of paintings by James Carroll Beckwith, ca. 50 engravings after drawings by William Rickarby Miller, prints after paintings by William Sidney Mount, and prints that belonged to George Henry Yewell. The miscellaneous graphic specimens include banknote engraving by Rawdon, Wright & Hatch; a graphotype, dated 1860; transfer prints on tissue to decorate plates with views of old New York; embroidery patterns; a drawing pattern book; prints from *Ariel;* European views after William H. Bartlett; non-New York material from the Isaccher Cozzens scrapbook; and early American prints collected by Hall Park McCullough.

Arrangement and access: Each section of the file has its own order. The general finding aid is a checklist of file categories. Another finding aid lists the Civil War envelopes by subject. The playing card decks are described individually on catalog worksheets.

References: Clipper ship cards are featured in Wendy Shadwell, "Commercial and Job Printing Serving the Maritime Industries," in *American Maritime Prints* (New Bedford, Mass.: Old Dartmouth Historical Society, 1985), pp. 95-129. Fraktur are described in Donald A. Shelley, "Illuminated Birth Certificates," *The New-York Historical Society Quarterly* 29 (April 1945): 92-105.

Related: The bulk of the Society's ephemera is in the Landauer Collection. The Reading Room has collections of broadsides, sheet music, trade catalogs, greeting cards, menus, and boxes of ephemera arranged by association with New York City events. The Department of Paintings, Sculpture, and Decorative Arts and the Manuscript Department also have material by or associated with Beckwith, Bryan, Durr, Magnus, Miller, Mount, and Yewell. The Department Museum has hand-drawn fraktur and the bulk of the Nadelman Collection.

Figure 53. *Broadway and 6th Avenue Junction, 33rd St. Elevated R.R. Station.* Pictorial lettersheet lithograph published by Charles Magnus, New York, ca. 1882. (Neg. no. 70806)

Charles Magnus combined two technologies to create an extensive series of pictorial lettersheets (stationery) with views of New York City. He started with a photograph to provide accurate perspective and architectural details, then added hand-drawn figures and vehicles to animate the scene, which was printed lithographically and often colored. Society staff notations identify and date various buildings in this view, which looks south toward the Union Dime Savings Bank in what is now Manhattan's Herald Square area.

80

23. NORVIN H. GREEN COLLECTION OF ELEVATED RAILROAD PHOTOGRAPHS

ca. 1890–1910 and ca. 1940.
ca. 60 albums (ca. 4,000 photographic prints, 5 × 7 in.);
ca. 300 loose prints (most 5 × 7 in.); and ca. 3,750 film negatives (most are 3½ × 2½ in., ca. 650 are 5 × 7 in.).

Business executive, civic leader, railroad enthusiast, and Society Trustee Norvin Hewitt Green (1894–1955) compiled a record of New York elevated railroads that focuses on the dismantling of most of the lines around 1940. Green hired the local advertising photography firm of H.F. Dutcher to document the demolition in almost 4,000 views. Street level businesses are revealed block by block as the heavy skeletal structure and stations are removed along Manhattan's Sixth Avenue line (1939) **(Figure 54)**, Ninth Avenue line (1940), and Second Avenue line (1941); and along Brooklyn's Fifth Avenue, Fulton Street, and Sands Street lines (1941). Brief captions identify each street address and date. Comments on girder weight, crane operation, and special demolition feats accompany the Brooklyn line views. A group of ca. 650 pre-demolition negatives shows all of the Manhattan lines, including the Third Avenue line, which was not dismantled until the mid-1950s. Green also gathered copies of historical views, which depict steam and electric engines, the Manhattan Railway Company, the Brooklyn Bridge railroad, and the Brighton and Sea Beach surface lines, ca. 1900–1910.

Figure 54. Elevated railroad demolition, station at Sixth Avenue and 33rd Street, New York City. Photograph by H.F. Dutcher, March 8, 1939. (Neg. no. 7891)

Images from different collections often can be combined to illustrate how an area changes over time. The elevated railroad in Figure 53, pictured when it was fairly new (ca. 1882), is being dismantled in this photograph taken in 1939.

Arrangement and access: Demolition survey prints are assembled in albums according to elevated line name and demolition date, except for the Sixth Avenue line, which is organized geographically. Corresponding demolition negatives are filed by Society-assigned numbers. Their jackets identify specific street locations and can be scanned to determine in which album a particular site appears. "Historical" views are in separate albums. Pre-demolition negatives lack corresponding prints. The finding aid summarizes the collection's contents.
Provenance: Gift from Norvin H. Green in 1940–1951.
Related: Many other elevated railroad views are in the Geographic File, including construction scenes from the 1800s.

24. GEORGE P. HALL & SON PHOTOGRAPH COLLECTION
ca. 1890–1920.
ca. 1,500 modern photographic prints (11 × 14 in. to 18 × 22 in.); ca. 100 glass negatives (most 11 × 14 in. to 18 × 22 in.); ca. 100 modern copy negatives (8 × 10 in.). Accompanied by photographer's logbook.

George P. Hall (1832–1900) apprenticed as a daguerreotypist in Ohio before founding the successful commercial photography firm of Geo. P. Hall & Son, which was active in the Manhattan and Brooklyn area from around 1875. His son, James S. Hall, continued the firm until about 1911. The company offered photographs for general sale and published many as illustrations in *King's Views of New York City* and in its own souvenir viewbooks. The Society has more than 1,000 Hall photographs, 1895–1911, which were printed in the 1970s from the original glass negatives. These large-format views are notable for their high-angle perspectives (Figure 55). They provide clear, detailed, and flattering depictions of many topics, including urban skylines and bridges, parks, hotel and theater exteriors, early skyscrapers, Coney Island, and the U.S. Navy's new steel battleships. There are also some photographs of the Hall business premises and of family members. A logbook documents the firm's work from ca. 1895 on and indicates which negatives were returned to clients when the firm closed. The Society added to the collection a few hundred modern prints it had made from large-format negatives taken ca. 1890 to 1920 by other photographers, among them John S. Johnston, the Langill Photo Company, and William J. Roege.

Arrangement and access: The prints are filed in one of the following categories: Manhattan (subdivided into building types, street scenes, and panoramic views); Brooklyn and Long Island; Staten Island; Outside New York City; Ships; and Miscellaneous. The finding aid is a list of filing categories, with an index to Manhattan buildings and streets. Many of the negatives have been indexed in the Negative File catalog.
Provenance: Glass negatives by Hall were purchased from James S. Hall in 1945, with later additions from other sources.
Related: Some vintage prints from Hall negatives can be found in the Geographic File.
At other institutions: The International Museum of Photography at the George Eastman House has almost 100 glass negatives by Geo. P. Hall & Son, donated to it by the Society in exchange for prints and copy negatives. The Museum of the City of New York also has negatives by Hall.

Figure 55. *Curb Brokers, Broad Street.* Modern print from glass negative by Geo. P. Hall & Son, N.Y., copyright 1912. (Neg. no. 59174)

The American Stock Exchange began with agents called curb brokers because they met their clients in the streets of Manhattan's financial district. The New York Curb Market moved indoors in 1921 and adopted its current name in 1953. In this view looking toward Wall Street, the New York Stock Exchange is the first building partially visible on the left.

Figure 56. *James K. Polk, 11th President of the United States.* On stone by A. Newsam; lithograph by P.S. Duval, published by C.S. Williams, Philadelphia, copyright 1846. (Neg. no. 70805)

The 11th president of the United States, James Knox Polk (1795-1849) was a Democrat from Tennessee. His capable administration (1845-1849) is known for several achievements including the expansion of United States territory to include Texas, California, and other western areas. Albert Newsam, a deaf-mute artist noted for his portrait lithographs, copied this particular likeness from another printmaker, Charles Fenderich.

25. HENRY O. HAVEMEYER COLLECTION OF PORTRAIT PRINTS OF AMERICAN STATESMEN
ca. 1790-ca. 1920, bulk ca. 1830-ca. 1900.
ca. 3,500 prints, chiefly engravings and lithographs.

Business executive Henry Osborne Havemeyer (1876-1965) was known as a discerning collector of Americana. He donated many kinds of material to the Society, which he joined in 1925 and served as a trustee from 1944 until his death. His special collection of portraits of American statesmen includes the presidents from Washington through Wilson, many of their vice presidents and cabinet officers, Supreme Court justices, and also Henry Clay, John C. Calhoun, Daniel Webster, and Winfield Scott. This portrait gallery of government leaders is a multifaceted research resource. By preserving numerous likenesses of certain people, Havemeyer provided material for studies in biography, iconography, popular culture, portraiture techniques, and printmakers' marketing practices. The estimated 700 portraits of Washington and 250 portraits of Lincoln are to be expected considering the long popularity of these presidents, and there are also nearly 300 images of Andrew Jackson. Commercial printmakers produced most of the likenesses as they competed to sell large quantities of attractive and accurate portraits derived from fine art paintings, from photographs, and from life. Represented artists, engravers and lithographers include Nathaniel Currier, Francis D'Avignon, James B. Longacre, Albert Newsam (Figure 56), Albert Rosenthal, and John Sartain. In addition to separately published engravings, lithographs, woodcuts, etchings, and photogravures, there are illustrations from books, patriotic portrayals on sheet music covers (Figure 57), and profiles on silk badges.

Arrangement and access: Small prints are filed chronologically by the sitter's term in office (or in some cases alphabetically by sitter's name) and then by item number within one of these categories: Presidents, Vice Presidents, Cabinet Officers, Supreme Court Justices, and Other. Large prints are housed in the Portrait File and are identifiable by a Havemeyer Collection number marking. The finding aid, a checklist of all prints by category and item number, provides brief descriptions or references to descriptions in published print catalogs.
Provenance: Gift from Henry O. Havemeyer in 1946-1952.
Related: Likenesses of most of the people can also be found in the Portrait File.

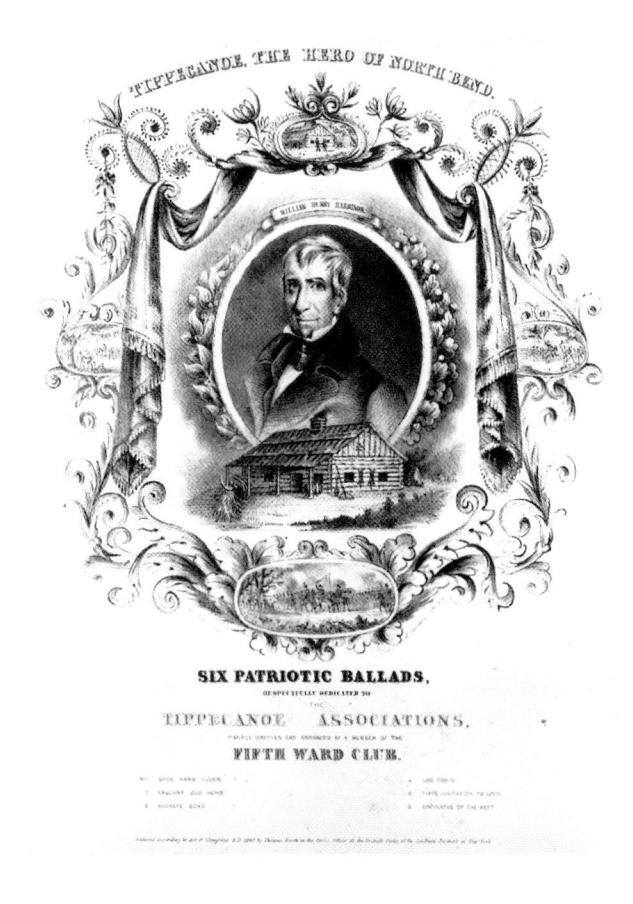

Figure 57. *Tippecanoe, the Hero of North Bend. Six Patriotic Ballads.* Sheet music cover, drawn by Charles Lewis, lithographed by N. Currier, New York, and copyrighted by Thomas Birch, 1840. (Neg. no. 64694)

When William Henry Harrison (1773-1841) ran for president in 1840, his Whig party created a huge public relations image campaign that swept him into office. They used songs and symbols, such as the log cabin shown here, to associate the aristocratic Harrison with soldier-farmer frontier values. Small vignettes on the sheet music reminded people of Harrison's victory over the Shawnee in an 1811 battle at the Tippecanoe River in Indiana. Nathaniel Currier, the lithographer of this sheet music, specialized in popular prints.

26. MATTIE E. HEWITT AND RICHARD A. SMITH PHOTOGRAPH COLLECTION

ca. 1910–1960, bulk 1920s–1930s.
ca. 4,000 photographic prints and 200 film negatives (8 × 10 in.).

Noted garden and architecture photographer Mattie Edwards Hewitt (died 1956) moved to New York City in 1909 to share a studio with Frances Benjamin Johnston. By the 1920s, she was working independently. When Hewitt retired to Boston, she left her working files to her nephew, Richard Averill Smith, who added to them many of his own prints. After Smith's death in 1971, the Nassau County Museum received more than 12,000 photographs and distributed many to various historical societies according to their geographic interests. The New-York Historical Society received material for approximately 485 assignments, most of them residences in Manhattan. Approximately three-quarters of the photographs are credited to Hewitt, and the remainder are by Smith. The bulk of the clients are popular magazines and interior decorators. Views of fashionable apartment interiors, newly built houses, small urban gardens, and other residential settings (Figure 58) display the work of decorators and the tastes of well-known people, among them designer Raymond Loewy and photographer Margaret Bourke-White. There are also interiors of hotels, restaurants, clubs, shops, and decorator exhibitions. Miscellaneous images include a 1940 "House of Ideas," a Vanderbilt family yacht, and a radio station. Captions are usually limited to client's name and address and are often dated. The decorator is identified for about half of the assignments.

Figure 58. Interior, residence of Hope Hampton, 1145 Park Avenue, New York City. Decorated by Elsie de Wolfe. Photograph by Mattie E. Hewitt, 1935. (Neg. no. 66069)

By photographing this Park Avenue residence, Hewitt both publicized and preserved interior decoration work credited to the noted Elsie de Wolfe (1865–1950). DeWolfe, after modest success as an actress, became an interior decorator in 1905. She was famous for encouraging women to take charge of decorating their homes. Her firm continued until the 1930s, although by 1920 she lived chiefly in France.

Arrangement and access: Prints are filed by the name of the resident or business. A finding aid lists each assignment by name, with indexes by decorator and building address.
Provenance: Gift from the Nassau County Museum in 1971.
References: *Portrait of an Era in Landscape Architecture: The Photographs of Mattie Edwards Hewitt* (Bronx, N.Y.: Wave Hill, 1983).

Figure 59. *America.* Engraving by Cornelis Visscher, ca. 1650-1660. (Neg. no. 53680)

The Dutch engraver Cornelis Visscher (ca. 1619-1662) borrowed the idea of representing America as a naked woman on an armadillo from earlier allegories. The inscription describes America as the strangest continent where people live as lawless cannibals in lands with gold and silver and parrots. The allegory underscores how little many Europeans knew about North and South America in the 1600s and how fascinated they were by an apparently rich and exotic territory.

27. JAMES H. HYDE COLLECTION OF ALLEGORICAL PRINTS OF THE FOUR CONTINENTS

ca. 1500-ca. 1900, bulk 1600-1800.
ca. 800 prints, chiefly engravings, some woodcuts and lithographs.

Philanthropist and francophile James Hazen Hyde (1876-1959) lived in France for many years and compiled an extensive collection of allegorical works portraying the four continents of Africa, America, Asia, and Europe. The theme was popular in the 1500s and 1600s as Europeans explored lands new to them. Hyde's prints, drawings, and decorative art objects were dispersed among several museums. The Society received about 500 allegorical prints, most of which feature

South and North America and complement descriptions of the "new" world in its map and book collections. These French, English, German, Italian, Dutch, Flemish, Spanish, and Portuguese prints typically personify America as an Indian huntress surrounded by such exotic animals as the armadillo and by other symbols of an intriguing land rich in natural resources (Figure 59). Also in the collection are prints from the 1700s and 1800s related to France and the United States, including a group honoring Benjamin Franklin, several caricatures of the American colonies, and popular prints from *Épinal.*

Arrangement and access: Prints are filed by general type and nationality. The finding aid lists broad categories and quantities of material. The caricatures are fully described in the Caricature and Cartoon File index.
Provenance: Gift from James H. Hyde in 1953 and 1957.
Related: The Manuscript Department has Hyde's correspondence, diaries, and other papers from 1891 to 1941.
At other institutions: The Metropolitan Museum of Art, the Brooklyn Museum, the National Gallery of Art, and the Cooper-Hewitt Museum also have material collected by Hyde representing the four continents. Hyde's reference photographs of works with the four continents theme are at the Cooper-Hewitt Museum; corresponding negatives are at the Library of Congress, Prints and Photographs Division.

28. FRANK M. INGALLS PHOTOGRAPH COLLECTION
ca. 1900–1930.
ca. 500 photographic prints and 1,035 negatives (285 glass and 750 film,
5 × 7 in. and smaller, including a few stereographs).

Frank M. Ingalls, an active amateur photographer from at least 1895–1930, wrote that he always carried a small camera with him, even when it rained, to be sure he never missed an unexpected opportunity. In a series of illustrated articles in the *American Annual of Photography,* 1906–1911, he advised his readers on the best equipment and sites for photographing New York City. He also published designs for a camera club's rooms based on his own 23rd Street Y.M.C.A. club experience. Among the most striking images at the Society are construction views of the Singer (Figure 60) and Metropolitan Life skyscrapers. Other photographs portray details of Manhattan street life: store windows, a push cart market, steam drills, snow removers, a female pretzel vendor, and flag-draped buildings and fireworks displays. Scenes on excursion steamboats, Coney Island, and the Kew Gardens railroad station in Queens provide glimpses of life beyond Manhattan. Ingalls identified each image by location and noted building names and interesting features such as kiosks. A few images are dated.

Figure 60. Singer Building under construction, 149 Broadway, New York City. Glass negative by Frank M. Ingalls, November, 1907. (Neg. no. 64200-400-31)

Architect Ernest Flagg designed the 47-story Singer Building, which was built in lower Manhattan in 1905–1908. Ingalls photographed the skyscraper near the end of its construction. Also under construction (to the left and right of the slender Singer tower), is the City Investing Building. In 1970, the demolition of the Singer Building helped fuel the landmarks' preservation movement.

Arrangement and access: Vintage and modern prints, representing about half of the negatives, are filed by Ingalls' original numbers. Photocopies of selected prints are in the Geographic File. The glass negatives are also filed by Ingalls' numbers and are indexed by subject, street name, and building name in the Negative File catalog, with a complete list under "Ingalls." The handwritten finding aid, received with the photographs, lists each image by number and also by such subject categories as Streets, Parades, Theatrical Advertising, and Miscellaneous.
Provenance: Gift from the photographer in 1943.

A SACRIFICE TO THE POLITICAL WOLF.
REPUBLICAN DESPERATION AND THE PERIL OF NEW YORK CITY.

Figure 61. *A Sacrifice to the Political Wolf. Republican Desperation and the Peril of New York City.* Color lithograph drawn by Joseph Keppler and published in *Puck,* October 29, 1884. (Neg. no. 70804)

Keppler despised Tammany Hall, the leading Democratic Party organization in New York City. In this cartoon, Keppler portrays Tammany Hall politicians as a hungry wolf ready to devour New York City (shown as a little girl) in a rumored deal that would give Tammany votes to the Republicans in exchange for patronage favors. The Republican presidential candidate James G. Blaine, also known as the "Plumed Knight," is riding in a sleigh drawn by horses labeled "bluster," "bribery," and "brag." Keppler supported Grover Cleveland, the Democratic nominee who won the 1884 presidential election shortly after this cartoon was published.

29. JOSEPH KEPPLER CARTOON COLLECTION

ca. 1860–1950, bulk 1875–1910.
ca. 350 cartoon chromolithographs, some black-and-white cartoon prints, and ca. 80 cartoon drawings. Accompanied by 4 photograph albums and ca. 50 loose photographs, ephemera, clippings, and a book.

A formally trained artist, Joseph Keppler (1838–1894) drew cartoons for *Kikeriki!* and was also a successful actor before he emigrated from Vienna to St. Louis in the late 1860s. After several theatrical and publishing ventures failed, Keppler moved to New York to work as a cartoonist for Frank Leslie's publications. In 1876, he and Adolph Schwarzmann launched his second *Puck*, a German weekly humor magazine. An English edition *Puck* soon followed and became one of the most influential journals in the United States during the 1880s. Keppler created many of its color cartoon covers and double-page center spreads. Other magazines followed his lead in chromolithograph illustration, and a generation of cartoonists trained under his eye. His finely drawn satires, often arranged as if theatrical stage scenes, ridiculed Ulysses S. Grant, James G. Blaine (the tattooed man), Benjamin Harrison, Tammany Hall Democrats (Figure 61), the tariff, prohibition, radical labor unions, and the Catholic Church, among other topics. He supported Grover Cleveland, civil service reform, and open immigration. His son, Udo Keppler (1872–1956), joined *Puck*'s staff in 1891, and changed his name to Joseph Keppler, Jr., after his father's death. Also a fine cartoonist, Udo contributed to *Puck* until the early 1910s, when he sold the magazine and concentrated on his interest in Native Americans. Most of the Society's collection relates to the senior Joseph Keppler. Included are several hundred chromolithograph proofs or tear sheets for *Puck;* some cartoons from *Leslie's* and other magazines; *Puck* imitations and ephemera; ca. 80 cartoon drawings by each Keppler, Frederick B. Opper, and Art Young; portrait photographs of Keppler family members, ancestors, and friends; programs from the senior Keppler's theatrical career in the 1860s–1870s; and the book *A Selection of Cartoons from Puck by Joseph Keppler, 1887-1893* (Keppler & Schwarzmann, 1893).

Arrangement and access: The material is grouped by format and creator, for example: Proofs for *Puck;* Drawings by Keppler, Jr., and Associates; Theater Programs. The photograph albums are housed in the Album File. Some family portraits and interiors of residences are in the Portrait File. The finding aid is a short description of each filing category.

Provenance: Most of the collection was donated by Mrs. Joseph Keppler, Jr., in 1956, with later additions. Other material was donated by Mr. and Mrs. Claude Brabyn in 1969.

References: Richard S. West, *Satire on Stone: The Political Cartoons of Joseph Keppler* (Urbana and Chicago: University of Illinois Press, 1988).

Related: Correspondence and other papers of both father and son are in the Manuscript Department. The Department of Paintings, Sculpture, and Decorative Arts has non-cartoon drawings and paintings by both men, the elder Keppler's death mask, and other material.

30. THERON W. KILMER PORTRAIT PHOTOGRAPH COLLECTION
ca. 1920s–1940s.
66 photographic prints; some are gum prints (13 × 10 in. or larger).

Theron Wendell Kilmer (1872–1946), a well-known New York pediatrician and police surgeon, pursued his photographic avocation by specializing in soft-focus head-and-shoulder portraits of men, most of whom were his colleagues. Kilmer won many prizes for his photographs of character-filled faces. He also published more than a dozen portraits and technical articles in the *American Annual of Photography* and in *Photo-Era*, to which he contributed from ca. 1915 until his death. About half of the Society's portraits depict physicians, clergymen, and other men identified by name. The remaining portraits are studies of African-American men, men with beards, and such character types as *The Sheik*. Most of the prints are signed and bear stickers from camera club exhibitions throughout the United States.

Arrangement and access: The prints are filed by numbers that correspond to brief undated captions on the checklist finding aid, which was received with the photographs.
Provenance: Gift in 1973.

31. BELLA C. LANDAUER COLLECTION OF BUSINESS AND ADVERTISING EPHEMERA
ca. 1700–present, bulk 1850–1920.
ca. 378,500 items: 350,000 items in scrapbooks; 10,000 loose items; 5,000 posters;
2,500 pieces of sheet music; 3,000 three-dimensional objects; 8,000 trade catalogs and pamphlets.
Accompanied by 90 reference books and extensive correspondence.

Known today as the first lady of ephemera, the energetic Bella Clara Landauer (1874–1960) began gathering what she fondly called scraps of old paper in the 1920s. She donated her early finds to the Society in 1926 and for more than 30 years made the growing collection available to researchers as she assembled a vast array of American trade cards, lottery tickets, handbills, labels, and countless other raw materials of history and popular culture. The Society continues to add to this premier ephemera collection primarily by building on its strength—New York material from the late-1700s to early-1900s. Commercial job printers produced most of the ephemera. Media range from rough woodcuts to elaborate chromolithographs and from fabric badges to watercolors. The smallest item may be Tom Thumb's miniature calling card; one of the largest is an advertisement painted on glass for men's and boys' fashionable clothing.

Figure 62. *Old Abe*. Advertisement for B. Leidersdorf & Co. chewing and smoking tobacco. Color lithograph by unidentified printmaker, ca. 1870. (Neg. no. 58502)

The Leidersdorf Company of Milwaukee, Wisconsin, used President Abraham Lincoln's name and face to promote its tobacco products.

Landauer sorted most of the ephemera by the product or service being promoted. Small items were mounted in large folio scrapbooks, often hinged so that both front and back of a piece are visible. There are also boxes and drawers filled with broadsides and posters, sheet music, trade catalogs, and such three-dimensional objects as tobacco tins, advertising fans, and souvenir paper weights. The largest collection categories reflect the most heavily advertised products and enterprises: clothing, patent medicines, dry goods, food and beverages, theatrical enterprises, tobacco items (Figure 62), and transportation. More specialized topics include asbestos, cryptography, electricity, penmanship, and slavery. The special sheet music section features pictorial covers depicting a variety of dances, women's suffrage themes, and New York City events and views. There is also a set of Bella Landauer's publications and her correspondence, which documents not only her own collection but the interests of other ephemerists, among them the noted British collector John Johnson. Extensive compilations of advertising ephemera received from other sources include rare

Figure 63. *Try Our Cable Screw Wire Boots & Shoes.* Chromolithograph trade card by Donaldson Brothers, New York City, ca. 1875. (Neg. no. 59085)

Construction of the Brooklyn Bridge began in 1869 to link Manhattan and Brooklyn across the East River. The bridge captured the graphic artists' imaginations long before it was completed in 1883. In this trade card advertisement, two shoes represent the bridge towers, and the wires used to attach soles and uppers are extended to form the bridge's suspension cables.

early American watchpapers, bookmarks (donated by Wattmann), unused cigar box labels (donated by Sydney Voice), cigarette packages, matchbook covers, and speakeasy cards (Introduction, Figure 17). More recent acquisitions include the 1870s sample book of small town job printer George H. Butler of Whitehall, New York; and material related to the 1986 Statue of Liberty centennial.

This pictorial miscellany can contribute to many research topics, from automatodeon (a steam calliope) to zylobalsamum (a hair dressing). The easiest queries to answer are those that parallel the collection's own categories—for example, information about hotels or cocaine-based medicines. Historians delight in images of business enterprises not otherwise documented. Archaeologists use china illustrations from billheads and price lists to help identify their finds. Studies of the Brooklyn Bridge benefit from ephemera which imaginatively demonstrates the bridge's symbolic appeal (Figure 63). The titles of Landauer's publications indicate other types of cultural and printing history that can be investigated: *The Indian Does Not Vanish in American Advertising, Literary Allusions in American Advertising as Sources of Social History,* and *Some Trade Cards with Particular Emphasis on the Currier and Ives Contributions.* Inquiries that seek a subject depicted in the ephemera (for example, baseball, working women, or ethnic stereotypes) or a type of ephemera (for example, calendars or early engraved trade cards) have been successfully pursued by discovering which advertisers featured particular themes and formats.

Arrangement and access: Most material is filed by storage format (ephemera mounted in scrapbooks, loose ephemera, posters, sheet music, pamphlets and books, three-dimensional objects) and then by the topic being advertised. Within some of the larger topic areas, there are further categorizations such as alphabetical groupings of companies. The finding aid is a checklist of the various filing categories and special indexes. These special indexes include a card description of each poster with cross references for printmakers. The sheet music is indexed by topic or musical style. Landauer's handwritten cross-reference volumes can be helpful in tracking down topics that cut across categories such as paper bags or interiors. The basic scrapbook categories are: Advertising; Agriculture; Animals; Antiques; Art; Aviation; Beverages; Building trades; Business; Clothing; Clubs and societies; Cotton; Dances and balls; Drugs; Dry goods; Electricity; Express companies; Food; Furniture; Hardware; Hotels and restaurants; Household; Insurance; Jewelry; Lawyers; Leather goods; Lotteries; Military; Oil; Optical; Packaging; Paper; Periodicals; Photography; Plastics; Printing, engraving and lithography; Professions and occupations; Publications; Radium, uranium, etc.; Real estate; Religion, philanthropy, and hospitals; Rubber; Schools and colleges; Seeds and plants; Sewing machines; Sports, toys, and games; Stationery and valentines; Stoves, furnaces, and ranges; Theatrical enterprises; Tobacco; Toilet articles and beauty aids; Transportation; Undertakers; United States government; Warehouses; Waterworks; Wool; World War II "E" awards to American industry.
Provenance: Gift from Bella C. Landauer, 1926–1960, with later additions from her son, James D. Landauer, and other sources.
References: A chronicle of her interests and bibliography of her 34 publications appear in Bella C. Landauer, "Collecting and Recollecting," *The New-York Historical Society Quarterly* 43 (July 1959): 334-349. Almost 100 posters are reproduced in Mary Black, *American Advertising Posters of the Nineteenth Century from the Bella C. Landauer Collection of The New-York Historical Society* (New York: Dover, 1976). *Cameo Cards & Bella C. Landauer* (Ephemera Society of America, 1992) reprints "Collecting and Recollecting" and lists recent subject categories.
Related: The Graphic Arts File, Certificate File, and Poster File have similar formats of material. Ephemera can also be found in the Manuscript Division collections. The Reading Room has collections of broadsides, sheet music, trade catalogs, greeting cards, menus, and boxes of ephemera arranged by association with New York City events. The Bookplate File has the Landauer Bookplate Collection.
At other institutions: Landauer collections at other institutions include: Walt Whitman music and printers' mottoes (New York Public Library); Eugene O'Neill material (Dartmouth College); aeronautical pictures (Library of Congress and National Air and Space Museum); European trade cards, French wine labels, and Japanese matchbox covers (Metropolitan Museum of Art).

32. RICHARD H. LAWRENCE PHOTOGRAPH COLLECTION
1886-1889, copied and printed in 1950.
202 copy film negatives (4 × 5 in.). Accompanied by 186 modern reference prints (8 × 10 in.).

Gentleman banker Richard Hoe Lawrence (1858-1936) pursued his antiquarian interests through active participation in the Grolier Club and in the Society of Iconophiles, which published prints illustrating Manhattan's iconography. Lawrence was also an early member of the Society of Amateur Photographers of New York. He produced numerous lantern slides and won a silver prize for hand camera work at the same Society show at which Robert Bracklow and Alfred Stieglitz also won awards. Of special interest are the photographs he took for Jacob Riis of slum conditions in Manhattan's Lower East Side in 1887. Lawrence and fellow camera club members Dr. John T. Nagle and Dr. Henry G. Piffard accompanied Riis until he learned to photograph on his own. Riis used the resulting lantern slides in his famous lectures on "The Other Half: How It Lives and Dies in New York." Maren Stange has recently shown that Lawrence took at least 31 of the photographs usually credited to Riis, but Lawrence cropped his copies to achieve softer character-type studies (Figure 64). Of the 37 slum views at the Society, five are credited to Piffard, who provided the necessary expertise in lighting dark alleys and interiors with the new magnesium flash powder technique. Other views show opium smokers in Chinatown, homeless lodgers and prisoners at a police station, a "black and tan" dive, and a boys' gang acting out a robbery.

Also significant are eight early action shots of baseball games at the Manhattan Polo Grounds in 1886 (Introduction, Figure 2). More routine views, possibly taken during family or camera club outings, include: beach bathing, the Blizzard of 1888, the 1889 Washington Inaugural Centennial naval and land parades, a fire, the Produce Exchange and Spanish Flats, sport shooting and tennis, house interiors, and Sing Sing prison. Lawrence captioned some of the photographs with descriptive titles and dates. Society staff devised short titles for the others and annotated the slum prints with detailed notes about comparable views by Jacob Riis.

Arrangement and access: Prints are filed by subject. Negatives are filed by Society-assigned numbers. The finding aid lists each image by key title subject word and by negative number. Some of the photographs are indexed in the Negative File catalog.
Provenance: Copied from lantern slides and albums on loan from the photographer's widow, Mrs. Jessie Cort Lawrence, in 1950.
References: Maren Stange, "From Sensation to Science: Documentary Photography at the Turn of the Century," in her *Symbols of Ideal Life* (New York: Cambridge University Press, 1989): 6-26.
Related: Similar slum images are in the Riis Reference Photograph Collection.
At other institutions: Several lantern slides credited to Lawrence are in the Riis Collection at the Museum of the City of New York.

Figure 64. Mulberry Bend, Mulberry Street, New York City. Print from lantern slide by Richard H. Lawrence, 1887. (Neg. no. 32308)

Lawrence cropped this photograph horizontally to emphasize the faces of the people in the notorious Mulberry Bend slum. When Jacob Riis published the photograph in his 1890 book, *How the Other Half Lives,* he called it *Bandit's Roost* and cropped it vertically to emphasize the narrow alley environment.

33. RANDALL J. LEBOEUF COLLECTION OF ROBERT FULTON PRINTS
ca. 1815–ca. 1920, bulk 1820–1860.
56 prints (chiefly engravings and lithographs), 2 watercolors, and 1 pencil sketch.

Lawyer Randall J. LeBoeuf, Jr., (1897–1975) spent 50 years assembling a large collection of correspondence, broadsides, books, china and glassware, prints, and drawings related to Robert Fulton (1765–1815) and steam-powered vessels. Most of the prints depict individual boats and ships built in the 1820s to 1840s, in the first generation after Fulton's pioneering work. The 20 general views of harbors and of naval expeditions also feature steamboats. The American, British, and French prints include Detroit in 1820 (showing *Walk-in-the-Water,* the first Great Lakes steamboat); *Burning of the U.S. Steam Frigate Missouri at Gibraltar, Aug. 26th, 1843;* and the *Splendid Iron Steam Ship the Rainbow.* Among the images more directly related to Fulton are several portraits, a view of his birthplace in Pennsylvania, and the *Launch of the Steam Frigate Fulton,* which Fulton designed in 1814 to defend New York's harbor against British attack. Of special interest is *A View of West-Point,* a rare contemporary lithograph by F. Berthaux showing Fulton's first steamboat in the Hudson River waiting for passengers, ca. 1810.

Arrangement and access: Images of steamboats are filed alphabetically by the names of the vessels, followed by general views of fleets and harbors and by portraits.
Provenance: Bequest from Randall J. LeBoeuf, Jr., in 1976, with additions from his widow.
Related: Numerous views of steamboats are also in the Subject File. Other portions of the LeBoeuf Collection are in the Reading Room, Manuscript Department, and Department of Paintings, Sculpture, and Decorative Arts. The Manuscript Department has extensive additional Fulton material.

34. EDWIN LEVICK STUDIO PHOTOGRAPH COLLECTION
ca. 1925–1940, bulk 1935–1938.
ca. 270 negatives (most film and some glass, 4 × 5 in. and 5 × 7 in.).

Edwin Levick (1868?–1929) specialized in spot news and marine photography. His New York City studio, staffed with some eight assistants, supplied illustrations for the rotogravure sections of several leading newspapers. Most of the Society's images date from the decade after Levick's death, when the studio continued to cover local news topics. Among the 20 negatives from ca. 1925 are views of baseball at Ebbets Field in Brooklyn, Pennsylvania Station interiors, Times Square at night, and Walter Chrysler's home. Almost 80 negatives record the 1938 Eagle

Figure 65. Eagle Pencil Co. strike, 14th Street and Avenue B, New York City. Film negative by Edwin Levick, June-July, 1938. (Neg. no. 62533)

In the same year that workers went on strike at the Eagle Pencil Co., President Franklin D. Roosevelt signed the Fair Labor Standards Act. This new law tried to help the work force during the Depression by establishing a minimum wage of 25 cents an hour, rising to 40 cents an hour.

Pencil Company strike (Figure 65). Other assignments from the 1930s include the Housewrecker's Union strike, a women's tennis tournament, movie theater marquees, radio opera broadcasts sponsored by General Motors, and Jimmy Durante as Santa Claus. Each image has a brief caption.

Arrangement and access: The negatives are arranged by photographer's assignment and indexed by subject in the Negative File catalog, with a complete list under "Levick."
Related: The Mariner's Museum, Newport News, Virginia, has many yachting, steamship, and other maritime photographs by Levick.

Figure 66. New York Stock Exchange. Etching by Kuhler, 1928. (Neg. no. 67797)

This etching, looking down on the intersection of Broad and Wall Streets in lower Manhattan, features the New York Stock Exchange (on Broad Street) with a flag flying on its roof. Architect George B. Post designed the original building, which opened in 1903 and was expanded by Trowbridge and Livingston in 1923.

35. HERMAN N. LIBERMAN COLLECTION OF WALL STREET PRINTS

ca. 1830–ca. 1945.
ca. 80 prints, chiefly etchings and engravings, a few color; also 2 drawings.

Herman N. Liberman (1910?–1973) became a member of the New York Stock Exchange in 1931. His interest in local history and buildings is apparent in his selection of prints depicting the Wall Street financial district from the late-1700s to the mid-1900s. Engravings from the 1830s to 1860s portray the first and second Merchants' Exchange. The majority of the later etchings feature the famous temple front of the New York Stock Exchange designed in 1903 by George B. Post (Figure 66). Of particular interest are New York Stock Exchange interiors by Childe Hassam and Joseph W. Golinkin. Among the other artists represented are: Karl Dehmann, Andrew Karoly, Nat Lowell, Joseph Pennell, Anton Schutz, and Thomas F. Simon.

Arrangement and access: A checklist names each printmaker. Major artists are cross-referenced in the Boyd Collection index. A photocopy of each print is available for ready reference.
Provenance: Gift in 1977.
Related: Artist prints of the Wall Street area are also in the James Boyd Collection.

Figure 67. New First Baptist Church, 249 West 135th Street, Harlem, New York City. Color negative by Herman N. Liberman, ca. 1970. (Neg. no. Liberman-135th St.)

36. HERMAN N. LIBERMAN PHOTOGRAPH COLLECTION
ca. 1940–1973, bulk 1966–1973.
8 albums (ca. 3,000 photographic prints, most color and 3 × 5 in.) and ca. 2,500 35mm color negatives. Accompanied by a few portraits of Liberman.

According to his obituary in *The New York Times,* stockbroker Herman N. Liberman (1910?–1973) spent seven years photographing houses of worship in Manhattan. He began at the Battery in 1966 and walked from east to west, moving north in a serpentine pattern while recording the street facade of every church, meetinghouse, synagogue, and temple along the way, until he reached the northern tip of the island in 1973. His four-volume pictorial census provides several color snapshots each of ca. 890 Buddhist, Christian, Hindu, Jewish, and Muslim houses of worship, which are identified by name and address (Figure 67). Liberman filled another three albums, called "New York City," with views of commercial and public buildings, in particular those in the Wall Street area, 1950s–1970s, and of the World Trade Center construction. In a single album, Liberman documented private residences near his home in upper Manhattan, 1942–1973.

Arrangement and access: "Houses of Worship" prints are mounted in albums in geographic order. The corresponding negatives are filed in the same sequence. Prints in the other albums are grouped by subject or date.
Provenance: Gift in 1977.

37. WILLIAM E. LIGHT COLLECTION OF NEW YORK CITY PHOTOGRAPHS
1880s.
63 photographic prints on 43 mounts (8½ × 6½ in. in. or smaller).

One or more unidentified photographers, probably amateurs, took these New York City views in the 1880s when simpler equipment opened photography to more part-time enthusiasts. Many of the views focus on people (Figure 68) and street activities in Manhattan's Union Square area: a coal man, nuns, shoeshine boys, children playing, men standing around, photographers, well-dressed women, carriages, and animals. Only a few images are dated, among them an 1886 New York Athletic Club running race, the Blizzard of 1888, and the 1889 Washington Inaugural Centennial parade. Beach scenes and views of rain, simulated snow fall, midnight, and rooftops complete the group.

Arrangement and access: The prints are filed by topic: Parades, People—Boys and Men, People—Women and Mixed, and Miscellaneous. Reference copies in the Geographic File provide subject access.
Provenance: Gift from William E. Light in 1981.

Figure 68. People in Union Square, New York City. Two photographs on one mount by unidentified photographer, ca. 1885. (Neg. no. 64186)

The man with a basket is standing in front of B.L. Solomon & Sons at 29 Union Square West. The boy is carrying two sculptural groups, probably plaster casts.

Figure 69. *Franklin's Island Light.* Albumen print by unidentified photographer, ca. 1890s. (Neg. no. 71095)

Maine has many lighthouses because of its rugged coast. The Franklin Island Light was built on Muscongus Bay near Portland.

38. LIGHTHOUSE PHOTOGRAPH AND PRINT COLLECTION
ca. 1860–1920.
ca. 400 photographic prints and 95 lithographs.

The Society's interest in documenting maritime activity related to New York attracted donations of general material about lighthouses and other navigation aids. A set of lithographs, printed by Julius Bien ca. 1860 for the U.S. Lighthouse Service, contains plans, sections, and elevations of lighthouse towers, buoys, and similar structures. A set of ca. 35 albumen prints depicts lighthouses in Maine in the late-1800s (Figure 69). The largest set of photographs appears to be official records of scattered lighthouses, equipment, and outbuildings along the New England and Middle Atlantic coast. At least one image shows a Great Lakes lighthouse. Most of the photographs are identified by structure name, date, photographer, and a plate number, but geographic location is rarely given.

Arrangement and access: Each group of prints and photographs is housed separately.
Provenance: The set of Maine photographs was donated by the Metropolitan Museum of Art in 1953. The remaining photographs were donated by the U.S. Coast Guard in 1946.

39. PIRIE MACDONALD PORTRAIT PHOTOGRAPH COLLECTION

1900–1942.
500 photographic prints (6 × 9 in. and 10 × 13 in.). Accompanied by job card file.

When Pirie MacDonald (1867–1942) moved his studio from Albany to New York City in 1900, he decided to photograph men exclusively. During the next 40 years, thousands of men prominent in industry, finance, literature, art, music, politics, and science sat for him. Dramatic lighting characterizes his soft-focus head-and-shoulder portraits, which are contact prints from glass negatives. MacDonald participated actively in photographic organizations and received many awards both in the United States and in Europe, including election as an Honorary Fellow of the Royal Photographic Society. In accordance with MacDonald's wishes, his negatives were destroyed after his death. Five hundred portraits were presented to the Society as a lasting record of his life's work. His daughter later donated MacDonald's job record card file that documents 6,000 commissions from his New York City years. Portraits of Arctic explorer Roald Amundsen, bibliophile George Arents, playwright Noel Coward, automobile manufacturer Henry Ford, cartoonist Thomas Nast, etcher Joseph Pennell, President Theodore Roosevelt, and Rabbi Stephen Samuel Wise are representative of the Society's holdings. There are also several self-portraits (Figure 70).

Figure 70. Self-portrait. Photograph by Pirie MacDonald, 1935. (Neg. no. 65018)

When Edna R. Bennett interviewed Pirie MacDonald for the 1942 *Annual of Photography*, she wrote that he was much admired for his technique. MacDonald agreed that technique is all-important, but added: "Suppose you could print the letters of the alphabet more perfectly than anyone else. But you have no ideas. Could you write? No! It is the same with photography. Of what use is technique if you have nothing to say?"

Arrangement and access: The portraits are filed by a sequential number according to size (small or large) and sitter's name. The finding aid is a copy of the exhibition catalog, which has been annotated to indicate the filing number. Entries are listed alphabetically by surname and include the sitter's occupation and the portrait date.
Provenance: Gift from the photographer's widow, Mrs. Pirie MacDonald, and from his daughter and son-in-law, Mr. and Mrs. Everett Tutchings in 1943.
References: *List of 500 Portraits of Men Made in New York City, 1900–1942, by Pirie MacDonald, Photographer-of-Men* (New York: The New-York Historical Society, 1943). Eleanor Logan, "The Pirie MacDonald Collection," *The New-York Historical Society Quarterly* 27 (April 1943): 39-42.
At other institutions: The Library of Congress, Prints and Photographs Division, has a set of ca. 300 portraits of men by MacDonald.

40. JOHN MCCOMB ARCHITECTURAL DRAWING COLLECTION

ca. 1750–ca. 1830, bulk 1800–1830.
ca. 500 architectural and engineering drawings in ink, graphite, and color wash; a few engravings.

After working for his builder-architect father, John McComb, Jr. (1763–1853) became the principal architect in New York City between 1800 and his retirement in the 1820s. The Society's collection features ca. 150 elevations, sections, plans, and detail drawings for New York City Hall, his foremost work (Figure 71). Joseph F. Mangin drew the French Neoclassical designs for their joint 1802 competition entry, which McComb developed during the decade-long construction. Few of the collection's other drawings are for fully identified commissions, although the original captions provide such interesting clues as "Panopticon plan for a prison for juvenile offenders, 200′ diamr. To be divided into six classes according to their good behaviour." Among the 100 church designs, 34 have been associated with specific New York City churches. Another 60 to 70 drawings depict townhouses and country houses. The 50 drawings for public buildings portray Government House, Park Theatre, Princeton Theological Seminary, Rickett's Equestrian Amphitheatre, Vanderlyn's Cyclorama Rotunda, the Washington Benevolent Society headquarters, an insane asylum, a hospital, and other structures. The few commercial buildings include a bakery, hotel, and sugar refinery. The 40 engineering drawings feature lighthouses at Cape Henry, Virginia, and Eaton's Neck, New York; sewers; machinery; and fortifications.

Figure 71. New York City Hall, Manhattan. Cross section. Wash drawing by Joseph Mangin and John McComb, Jr., 1802. (Neg. no. 18988)

Architects Joseph Mangin and John McComb, Jr., prepared the set of drawings that won the City Hall design competition. This cross section shows a spiral stair leading to a Corinthian-columned room, which was used as the City Council Chamber. The two-story City Hall was built in 1803–1812 and through careful preservation still serves its role in lower Manhattan in a park off Broadway.

In addition, there are some 60 decorative designs; studies and school problems; sketches of buildings designed by other people; hand-drawn copies of real estate maps; drawings attributed to John McComb, Sr., to his relatives, and to Jacob Lawrence; and engravings by Giambattista Piranesi and others. Together with the account books, correspondence, and other material in the Manuscript Department, the collection provides an important resource for studying early architectural practices in the United States as well as documentation of specific structures, only a few of which survive.

Arrangement and access: New York City Hall drawings are filed by number and described in that sequence in a logbook compiled by a McComb descendant. The remaining drawings are filed in a separate numerical series, with drawings for similar projects sometimes grouped together. A card index describes most of these drawings by building type. A checklist describing all of the drawings in numerical sequence, with an alphabetical index, provides additional access to the collection. A database catalog is being compiled.
Provenance: Gift from Daniel Parish, Jr., in 1898, with small additions in 1902, 1905, and 1923, and gifts from McComb descendants Helen A. Collingwood in 1930 and Abbie C. Miller in 1949.
References: Agnes A. Gilchrist, "Notes for a Catalogue of the John McComb (1763-1853) Collection of Architectural Drawings in The New-York Historical Society," *Journal of the Society of Architectural Historians* 28 (Oct. 1969): 201-210. Agnes A. Gilchrist, "John McComb, Sr. and Jr., in New York, 1784-1799," *Journal of the Society of Architectural Historians* 31 (Mar. 1972): 10-21. Damie Stillman, "Artistry and Skill in the Architecture of John McComb, Jr." (Master's thesis, University of Delaware, 1956).
Related: More than 250 items by John McComb, Jr. and Sr., are in the Manuscript Department.

41. BURR MCINTOSH PHOTOGRAPH COLLECTION
ca. 1900–1910.
ca. 3,000 modern photographic prints (5 × 7 in., 8 × 10 in., and 11 × 14 in.); ca. 600 glass negatives (4 × 5 in. and 8 × 10 in.).

Known as "the cheerful philosopher," Burr McIntosh (1862–1942) distinguished himself in many careers, including those of actor, reporter, publisher, lecturer, cinematographer, and radio pioneer, as well as photographer. While many of these endeavors were short-lived, they gained him prestige and popularity among the stylish set. From 1903 to 1910, McIntosh produced *The Burr McIntosh Monthly*, which offered portraits of theater idols, scenes at fashionable athletic events, picturesque genre and nature studies, and discussions of photography as art. He moved to California when the magazine folded. The Society has the major collection of McIntosh's photographs. It

Figure 72. Woman and children playing a game, possibly blindman's bluff. Photograph by Burr McIntosh, ca. 1905. (Neg. no. 61618)

includes some early work—images from the Spanish-American War siege of Santiago, Cuba, which he covered for *Leslie's Weekly* and published as *The Little I Saw of Cuba.* Another series shows Secretary of War William H. Taft's good will trip to the Philippines in 1905. Most of the images are society and celebrity portraits, and many were published in McIntosh's magazine. Actors Ethel and John Barrymore appear at the seashore; philanthropist A.G. Vanderbilt celebrates a holiday at his Adirondack lodge; ingenue Evelyn Nesbit poses seductively; and architect Charles F. McKim enjoys a quiet country outing. Children playing (Figure 72), theatrical groups, and miscellaneous buildings complete the file. Caption information is usually limited to the sitter's name. The Society printed ca. 3,000 of the negatives in the 1940s; some of the remaining negatives also have prints.

Arrangement and access: Prints are filed by size, and within size, alphabetically by name of sitter. Unidentified people are filed as Children, Female, Male, and Groups. Other subjects are under Miscellaneous. The finding aid is an alphabetical list of sitters according to print size and indicates the number of prints available.
Provenance: Gift from the *New York Herald Tribune* in 1942.
At other institutions: The Library at the University of Washington has a substantial number of McIntosh photographs.

42. MCKIM, MEAD & WHITE ARCHITECTURAL RECORD COLLECTION

ca. 1875-ca. 1950, bulk 1890-1930.

ca. 48,000 architectural drawings, including ink on linen, blueprints, and other media; ca. 600 packages of detail drawings and specifications; ca. 1,500 photographs, including prints and glass and film negatives; ca. 20 photograph albums; ca. 650 boxes of correspondence; ca. 50 ledgers, including 17 bill books (1878-1947), 10 cash books (1894-1944), 8 contract books (1903-1930), and 9 journals (1882-1942); ca. 10 scrapbooks and 100 folders of clippings; and more than 300 original drawings for the *Monograph*.

Architects Charles Follen McKim (1847-1909) and William Rutherford Mead (1846-1928) shared an office in New York City in the early 1870s. When their brief association with William Bigelow ended in 1879, Stanford White (1853-1906) became their new partner. The firm quickly won national acclaim for visually pleasing, well-built structures, many of which combined imposing classical exteriors with richly decorated interiors. McKim and White, the chief designers, trained with noted architect Henry H. Richardson. McKim also studied at the Ecole des Beaux-Arts in Paris. Mead, who studied with architect Russell Sturgis and in Florence, supervised construction work and the large staff. McKim, Mead & White commissions at the Society include Shingle Style, Colonial Revival, and other country houses in Newport, Rhode Island (Figure 73); urban residences such as the Villard Houses, New York; and several structures at the World's Columbian Exposition in Chicago and on the Columbia and Harvard college campuses. Among the public facilities are Madison Square Garden, New York; Boston Public Library; Rhode Island State Capitol; Prospect Park entrances, Brooklyn, New York; Pierpont Morgan Library, New York; and Pennsylvania Station, New York. The Interborough Rapid Transit Powerhouse, New York, and the restoration of the University of Virginia rotunda represent less typical projects. After 1909, William M. Kendall, William S. Richardson, and other junior partners carried on the firm's work with such commissions in New York City as the Central Post Office, the Hotel Pennsylvania, and the Racquet and Tennis Club.

The Society's archive contains extensive documentation of the firm's operations and of individual buildings (Introduction, Figure 15). Original drawings, blueprints, and other material are available for some 1,000 commissions, although most information about the firm's early years is provided by photograph albums, clipping scrapbooks, and financial ledgers. The early careers of many architects who trained at the firm, for example, Henry Bacon, can also be studied. Line drawings made to illustrate *A Monograph of the Works of McKim, Mead & White, 1879-1915* represent the firm's major commissions.

Figure 73. Rosecliff, Newport, R.I. Pen and ink drawing by McKim, Mead & White, ca. 1900. (Neg. no. MMW-1286)

In 1898, Theresa Fair Oelrichs commissioned a summer cottage from architect Stanford White. The mansion, now a house museum, was modeled after a palace built for Louis XIV at Versailles. White's graceful ornamentation appears clearly in this drawing. The collection includes about 40 drawings for Rosecliff.

Arrangement and access: Material is filed by format and within each format is either alphabetical by project name or chronological. Separate checklist or card inventory finding aids, often limited to project names, cover: drawings donated in 1950; drawings donated in 1968; specifications and detail drawings; correspondence; negatives; packages of photographs; packages of clippings; photograph albums and scrapbooks; financial records.
Provenance: Gift from Lawrence Grant White, Stanford White's son, in 1950, with additions from Mrs. James Kellum Smith in 1968.
References: Wayne Andrews, "McKim, Mead and White: New York's Own Architects," *The New-York Historical Society Quarterly* 35 (Jan. 1951): 86-96. Leland Roth, *The Architecture of McKim, Mead & White, 1870-1920: A Building List* (New York: Garland, 1978).
Related: Stanford White family letters are in the Manuscript Department.
At other institutions: The Avery Architectural and Fine Arts Library at Columbia University also has Stanford White correspondence; Columbia campus plans; and many of the firm's scrapbooks, photograph albums, and miscellaneous record books. The Library of Congress, Manuscript Division, has Charles F. McKim's papers. Material may also be found in many other organizations including the archives of the firm's large institution clients.

Figure 74. Parkchester, Metropolitan Life Insurance housing project under construction, Bronx, New York. Film negative by McLaughlin Air Service, June 3, 1940. (Neg. no. 60912-17189)

The Parkchester housing project, built in the eastern Bronx between 1938 and 1942, filled a site of almost 130 acres. The Metropolitan Life Insurance Company sponsored the development. This city within a city was planned for 40,000 residents and offered many stores (including an early branch of Macy's) and easy access to the subway, which is visible where it runs above ground in the photo (right center). The buildings, from seven to 13 stories tall, contained more than 12,000 units and were spread among four landscaped quadrants.

43. MCLAUGHLIN AIR SERVICE PHOTOGRAPH COLLECTION
ca. 1935–1970, bulk 1940–1942.
ca. 700 film negatives and 75 prints (most 5 × 7 in., others 7½ × 9½ in.).

The Manhattan-based McLaughlin Air Service photographed sites throughout the New York City region in low altitude, oblique-angle aerial views. The Society acquired many images of the Bronx, Brooklyn, Queens, and Manhattan, as well as a few views of Staten Island and the New Jersey waterfront of the Hudson River. The majority of the photographs were taken in 1940–1942 and record the city before it underwent its post World War II development. Urban geography patterns stand out clearly as do such features as bridges, tunnels, roads, and housing projects (Figure 74). Subjects represented in more than 10 images include LaGuardia airport, the ocean liner Normandie, New York Central Railroad yards, and areas along the Hudson River and along East River Drive. More than half the photographs are captioned with specific locale and date. The remaining images are not identified beyond borough name.

Arrangement and access: Most of the negatives are filed chronologically by McLaughlin's job numbers. The remainder are grouped by borough name. The few prints are in the Geographic File under "Borough name—Aerial—McLaughlin." The finding aid is a subject checklist of the negatives, many of which are also indexed in the Negative File catalog by broad topics.
Provenance: Purchase from McLaughlin Air Service in 1972.

44. GEORGE W. MURDOCK COLLECTION OF STEAMBOAT PHOTOGRAPHS

ca. 1830-1940.

9 albums (ca. 1,800 photographic prints) and some loose prints. Accompanied by 2 albums of boat history clippings.

Marine engineer George Washington Murdock (1853-1940) grew up along the Hudson River and served on such famous steamboats as the *Mary Powell*. In his lifelong devotion to steamboat history, Murdock collected artifacts and compiled reference albums that depict Hudson River steamboats in broadside views, at piers (Figure 75), with crews, or after accidents. Handwritten histories accompany many illustrations, and there are copies of almost 200 of his newspaper articles about individual boats. Murdock filled other albums with pictures of steamboats that operated in Long Island Sound, New York City ferryboats, and miscellaneous vessels. Many of the photographs are copies of earlier photographs, prints, or paintings.

Arrangement and access: The photographs are mounted (sometimes alphabetically by boat name) within the following album categories: Hudson River steamboats, Long Island Sound steamboats, Ferries, and Miscellaneous. A card catalog indexes vessels in albums 1-7 by boat name. The Society has made copy negatives of many of the images, which are indexed in the Negative File catalog by boat name. Unmounted ferryboat photographs are also in the Subject File.
Provenance: Bequest and purchase from Murdock's estate in 1941.
Related: Additional steamboat images are in the LeBoeuf Collection, Scanlon Collection and Subject File. The Department of Paintings, Sculpture, and Decorative Arts has paintings and artifacts collected by Murdock.

Figure 75. *Boat Landing, Kingston, N.Y.* Photograph by Detroit Publishing Co., ca. 1905. (Neg. no. 16812)

The Detroit Publishing Company included Hudson River scenes, such as this one, among its nationally distributed photographs. George W. Murdock attached his own caption: "This picture shows the steamboat *New York* after being lengthened in 1897, landing at Kingston Point."

611. ICE MOUNTAIN, NIAGARA FALLS.

45. NEGATIVE FILE

1500–present, bulk 1850–1950.
More than 80,000 glass and film negatives, most black-and-white and some color (most 4 × 5 in. or 8 × 10 in., some as small as 35mm or as large as 30 × 40 in.).

Both original negatives (Cover illustration) and copy work have been added to this file since it was established in the 1910s. Most of the significant bodies of original material with corresponding prints (for example, the calotypes by Victor Prevost) are described in separate guide entries. Representative groups of other original views and portraits, include: scenes from the 1889 Washington Inauguration Centennial celebration; commercial views taken by John S. Johnston, ca. 1890 (Figure 76), by Hermann N. Tiemann, ca. 1900, and by William J. Roege, ca. 1920; daytime and nighttime snapshots of the 1939–1940 World's Fair by Harry Cotterell, Jr.; and ca. 20 panoramic film negatives, including views of the East River and Catskill Mountain resorts. Most of the copy work was made by staff photographers to document the Society's collections. The mixture of original and copy work in a single file with a single subject index provides a valuable, central illustration reference source for material in many Society departments—from broadsides, maps, and newspaper headlines to portrait paintings, fire equipment, lithographs, photographic prints, and unprinted negatives. This file is the first place to check for the Society's best-known and previously published images.

Arrangement and access: Negatives are filed by sequential numbers that reflect the cataloging dates. Original photographers' numbers are sometimes preserved as suffixes to the Society-assigned number (e.g., 61005-B320). A card catalog indexes subjects, although some museum objects are listed only under such general categories as "Silver" or "Furniture." Cataloging done before 1970 usually emphasizes subject matter and does not always describe photographers' names, dates, and media.
Related: Cohesive groups of negatives, chiefly those with corresponding prints, are described in separate entries and can be found under "Negatives" in the guide index. Any corresponding prints for the original negatives described above have usually been dispersed by topic in the Geographic, Portrait, or Subject files.

◀ Figure 76. *Ice Mountain, Niagara Falls.*
Glass negative by John S. Johnston, ca. 1890.
(Neg. no. 62071)

46. NEW-YORK HISTORICAL SOCIETY PICTORIAL ARCHIVE

ca. 1810–present, bulk 1930–1950.
ca. 1,000 photographic prints and 1,000 negatives; ca. 300 architectural drawings; several prints, certificates, and posters.

The Society's pictorial records of its own history illustrate the development of one of United States' oldest libraries and museums, founded in 1804. The archive also provides images of general interest to anyone investigating such topics as how paintings and historical artifacts were displayed to the public in the 1800s or state-of-the-art facilities in the 1930s. Coverage of Society activities is uneven. Representing the earliest years are a woodcut broadside commissioned from Alexander Anderson to commemorate the first St. Nicholas celebration in 1810 and the membership certificate designed by Louis Simond and engraved by Asher B. Durand in 1820. The archive also contains photographs and architectural drawings for the Society's first independent headquarters, built on Second Avenue in the 1850s (Figure 77), and for its current home on Central Park West, designed in 1901 by York and Sawyer and expanded in the 1930s (Introduction, Figure 10). An estimated 400 negatives document the archaeological work of the Field Exploration Committee (formed in 1918) and its members, who excavated American Revolution and War of 1812 sites in New York City and State from ca. 1900 to 1940, under the direction of William L. Calver.

Arrangement and access: Photographic prints are filed by subject: Buildings, Events, Collections, Public Programs and Education, Seals and Medals, Staff, Directors and Trustees. The finding aid is a checklist of filing categories. Negatives, architectural drawings, certificates, and posters are incorporated in the special files and indexes for those formats.

References: Many facilities, leaders, and artifacts from 1804 to the mid-1900s are illustrated in R.W.G. Vail, *Knickerbocker Birthday: A Sesqui-Centennial History of The New-York Historical Society* (New York: The Society, 1954). The Field Exploration Committee work is described in William L. Calver, *History Written With Pick and Shovel* (New York: The Society, 1950).

Related: The Archives Department maintains the bulk of the Society's archive: correspondence, minutes, accession logs, and scrapbooks. The Reading Room has a set of Society publications.

Figure 77. Proposed design for The New-York Historical Society headquarters on Second Avenue at 11th Street, New York City. Ink and watercolor drawing by Carstensen and Gildemeister, architects, 1854. (Neg. no. 64109)

In the 1850s, the Society built its own headquarters in lower Manhattan. Architects Georg J.B. Carstensen and Charles Gildemeister, who had recently designed New York's Crystal Palace, submitted this lively design for a multicolored building. The Society selected, however, a two-story, sandstone "Italian-Roman-Doric" structure by architects Mettam & Burke.

Figure 78. *Action between the Constellation and L'Insurgent, on the 9th February 1799.* Aquatint drawn, engraved, and published by Edward Savage, Philadelphia, May 20, 1799. (Neg. no. 41673)

A victory by the newly formed United States Navy inspired Edward Savage (1761-1817) to create this print and a companion view while the naval action was still recent news. The two, now very rare prints, are thought to be the earliest aquatints (an elaborate printmaking process) by a native artist. The American frigate *Constellation* captured the French ship in the West Indies, because the French were raiding American ships.

47. IRVING S. OLDS COLLECTION OF NAVAL PRINTS
ca. 1600-1950, bulk 1770-1850.
ca. 450 prints, chiefly engravings, also etchings, lithographs, aquatints, mezzotints, and woodcuts.
Accompanied by pamphlets, clippings, and lecture notes.

Prominent corporate lawyer Irving Sands Olds (1887-1963) was the chairman of U.S. Steel from 1940 to 1952 and also served as a trustee and president of The New-York Historical Society. Olds' interest in history focused on American pre-Civil War naval engagements and commanders, especially the young navy's prowess in the War of 1812. Olds collected some 1,150 prints, paintings, silhouettes, maps, broadsides, and decorative textiles from which the Society selected about 550 items, including more than 400 naval prints (many hand-colored) and several rare New York City views and large Currier & Ives scenes. The earliest naval event depicted is the British capture of Louisbourg, Canada, during the French and Indian War. The bulk of the prints portray naval actions during the Revolutionary War and during the War of 1812, with an emphasis on dramatic battles made famous in the slogans of heroic captains. Numerous American, British, and French prints show such American triumphs as John Paul Jones' *Bon Homme Richard* attacking the British *Serapis* in 1779 ("I have not yet begun to fight"), the *Constitution's* defeat of the *Guerriere* in 1812, and Oliver H. Perry's victory at the Battle of Lake Erie in 1813 ("We have met the enemy and they are ours"). Views of American defeats include the death of Captain James Lawrence when the British *Shannon* captured his *Chesapeake* in 1813 ("Don't give up the ship").

Many of the prints are based on eyewitness sketches and are thought to be accurate portrayals. Public interest in the dramatic naval actions can be gauged from the speed with which several of the prints were issued. For example, Thomas Birch and William Strickland published an aquatint of the American *Peacock* capturing the British *L'Epervier* within three months of the event in 1814. Other prints are more generalized commemoratives, including those issued by Nathaniel Currier and by the Kelloggs in the 1840s. Portraits of naval figures are plentiful. There are also several American and British caricatures and school sheets bordered with naval vignettes on which students wrote out poems. Of special interest to printmaking historians are such milestone pieces as the first historical aquatints prepared in the United States (Figure 78)—evidence of the country's growing technical and aesthetic sophistication. There are often several states of the same prints, which provides opportunities to study stages of print production.

Arrangement and access: Prints are filed by Olds Collection number. The first 250 prints are grouped chronologically according to naval engagement, with separate sections for New York City views, privateer actions, portraits, and miscellaneous scenes. The rest of the prints are in an inventory sequence. The finding aid is a copy of *American Naval and Other Historical Prints* and its two unindexed supplements, annotated to show the Society's holdings. The main book provides an artist, printer, and publisher index for approximately half of the prints. A card catalog describes most of the prints. The clippings and other supplemental material are available in a reference file.
Provenance: Bequest from Irving S. Olds in 1963.
References: Prints from no. 1 through 1138 are listed in Irving S. Olds, *American Naval and Other Historical Prints and Paintings, Including Portraits of American Naval Commanders and Some Early Views of New York* (New York, 1951, with supplements ca. 1955 and 1962). Prints from no. 1 through 500 are in Irving S. Olds, *Bits and Pieces of American History: As Told By a Collection of American Naval and Other Historical Prints and Paintings, Including Portraits of American Naval Commanders and Some Early Views of New York* (New York, 1951). Many prints are illustrated.
Related: Numerous naval prints are also in the Subject File. The Olds Collection broadsides, maps, manuscripts, paintings, and decorative art works are in the Reading Room, Manuscript Department, and Department of Paintings, Sculpture, and Decorative Arts, respectively.

Figure 79. Demolition of part of the glass-covered train concourse, Pennsylvania Station, New York City. Negative by Alexander Hatos, Dec. 30, 1965.
(Neg. no. Hatos-1965 Dec. 30)

48. PENNSYLVANIA STATION DEMOLITION PHOTOGRAPH COLLECTION

1951–1970, bulk 1964–1967
ca. 903 prints (5 × 7 in.) with corresponding 35mm negatives;
ca. 50 snapshot prints (various sizes);
9 enlarged prints (8 × 10 in.);
28 negatives (1½ × 2 in.).

McKim, Mead & White designed Pennsylvania Station as a majestic threshold for Manhattan travelers. Completed in 1910, this magnificent monument to railroad transportation filled the blocks from Seventh to Eighth Avenues, between 31st and 33rd Streets. Little more than 50 years later, the Pennsylvania Railroad Company decided to replace the vast glass-covered train concourse and vaulted waiting room with a new Madison Square Garden entertainment center and office complex. Despite public protest, demolition began in late 1963. Railroad employee Alexander Hatos chronicled the destruction between March 30, 1964, and June 13, 1967 (**Figure 79**). His black-and-white photographs document the dismantling procedures in detail. The loss of this civic masterpiece speeded the creation of the New York City's Landmarks Preservation Commission. In *Lost New York,* Nathan Silver quotes from *The New York Times* (October 30, 1963): "And we will probably be judged not by the monuments we build but by those we have destroyed."

Arrangement and access: Prints are arranged by date in 3-ring binders.
Provenance: Purchase, Gladys Zurkow, 1991.
Related: The McKim, Mead & White Architectural Record Collection contains some documentation on the station's construction.

Figure 80. *The Sir Roger de Coverley (Quadrille d'Honneur) at the New-Year's Ball in the Metropolitan Opera-House.* Drawn by T. de Thulstrup. Wood engraving from *Harper's Weekly,* January 18, 1890, p. 48. (Neg. no. 65218)

Artist Thure de Thulstrup (1848–1930) portrayed elegantly dressed couples celebrating the New Year by dancing a quadrille at an opera house, which opened in 1883 on Broadway in New York City. Ball manager Ward McAllister arranged the event for nearly 1,200 members of New York "society." The stage and auditorium were decorated with evergreens, wreaths, and flowers for what *Harper's Weekly* described as "the most brilliant and successful social event in the history of New York City."

49. HARRY T. PETERS COLLECTION OF PICTORIAL NEWSPAPER ILLUSTRATIONS
ca. 1845–1920, bulk 1860–1890.
ca. 10,500 prints, chiefly wood engravings, also woodcuts and halftone prints.

A successful coal merchant and avid sportsman, Harry Twyford Peters (1881–1948) is best known for his pioneer collecting and writing in the field of historical American lithography, especially Currier & Ives prints. His collection of 10,000 wood engravings from pictorial newspapers also reflects his interest in images that depict daily life and news events. Pictorial newspapers first appeared in the United States in the 1850s, modeled on the *Illustrated London News.* These weekly national publications had the time and resources to provide illustrated stories, which were unavailable in daily papers until the introduction of rapid photomechanical processes in the late-1800s. Most of the collection's single- and double-page sheets are from the leading American pictorial journals: *Frank Leslie's Illustrated Newspaper* and *Harper's Weekly* (Introduction, Figure 5). Other publications include *Gleason's Pictorial Drawing Room Companion* (later called *Ballou's Pictorial*), the *New York Illustrated News,* and *Scientific American.* The black-and-white engravings range from skilled eyewitness illustrations to dramatized inventions of a wide range of topics. New York City, home of many illustrated weeklies, appears in several thousand prints about banking, bridges, clubs, fires, journalism, law enforcement, markets, and winter activities (Figure 80). Many other major American cities and regions and some foreign places are also depicted. Numerous artists are represented, but except for works by W.M. Cary, A.B. Frost, Winslow Homer (ca. 200 prints), Thomas Nast (cartoons), Howard Pyle, and Frederic Remington, their prints are dispersed by subject.

Arrangement and access: Prints are grouped by topics within five broad categories: General Subjects; Art (including cartoons and prints by selected artists); Places; Sports; and New York City. The General Subject topics are: Animals; Black life; Children; Chinese life; Civil War; Coaching; Colonial life; Country life; Cowboys; Disasters; Entertainment; Fashions; Holidays; Hospitals, homes, and prisons; Immigration and emigrants; Indians; Industry and labor; Leisure; Liquor and temperance; Marriage, romance, and family; Military; Monuments; Occupations; Politics; Portraits; Poverty; Railroads; Religion, spiritualism, and witchcraft; Restaurants, food vendors, and food; School; Science; Ships; Sleighs; Transportation; Travel customs; Trials and meetings; Whaling; Women; and Miscellaneous. The finding aid is a list of all filing categories. Photocopies are available for ready reference.
Provenance: Gift from Harry T. Peters in 1946, with later additions from other sources.
Related: The Reading Room has entire volumes of many illustrated newspapers and magazines.
At other institutions: The Museum of the City of New York has the Peters Collection of Currier & Ives prints. The National Museum of American History, Division of Domestic Life, has the Peters *America on Stone* Lithography Collection.

Figure 81. Times Square, New York City. Photograph by Andreas Feininger, 1940. (Neg. no. 66834)

When noted photographer Andreas Feininger (born 1906) published *New York in the Forties,* he included this lively Manhattan night scene. The car, the Broadway marquees, and the Willkie Club signs (far right) all reflect a specific time period—autumn 1940. At the RKO Palace, James Cagney stars in the movie *City for Conquest.* The newsreels and short films at the Embassy include a new war documentary, *London Can Take It,* which showed English resilience during German bombing raids. On the same marquee are the names of opposing presidential candidates Franklin Delano Roosevelt (FDR) and Wendell Willkie, as well as Lew Lehr, a comedy newsreel commentator.

50. PHOTOGRAPHER FILE

ca. 1940–present.
ca. 1,000 photographic prints, most black-and-white and some color (most 11 × 14 in. or larger).

The file presents some 35 different photographers' views of New York City buildings and people from ca. 1940 to the present. Most images were donated by or purchased from the photographers, often for use in exhibitions. Photographers represented by numerous prints include: Alexander Alland (135 images of Black Jews in Harlem and Russian Gypsies on the Lower East Side, 1940); Bill Cunningham (90 portraits of models posed in period costumes in front of historic buildings, 1970s); Andreas Feininger (300 New York City scenes, 1940s and 1970s–1980s) (Figure 81); Robert Gambee (225 Manhattan seascapes, 1970s); Morris Huberland (50 images of New York City street life, 1940s–1950s); and Chris Mackey (25 Lower East Side street scenes, 1970s–1980s). Among the other photographers are Bill Aron, Rhoda Galyn, Michael George, Ruth Orkin, Leon Supraner, Lewis F. White, and William Winter.

Arrangement and access: Prints are filed by photographer's name. Entries in the Photographer's Reference Index identify each photographer and briefly describe the images. Checklists itemize the works by Alexander Alland and Morris Huberland.
Restrictions: The photographer's permission is usually required to reproduce the images.

51. CALVIN POLLARD ARCHITECTURAL DRAWING COLLECTION

ca. 1820–ca. 1850.
ca. 75 sheets and 2 albums of architectural and engineering drawings, chiefly elevations and floor plans in ink, graphite, and color wash.

Calvin Pollard (1797–1850) began as a builder in New York City ca. 1820, then emphasized his design talents by listing himself as an architect in city directories from 1840 until his death. Despite the fact that few clients or specific locales are identified and only about 10 drawings are signed or dated, the rarity of original designs from this time period makes the Society's drawings valuable. For example, plans for some 15 residential projects provide data for studying the development of the typical New York house (Figure 82). Other designs have been classified as business establishments, churches, and such public buildings as a lunatic asylum. One album contains contract drawings to reconstruct the New National Theatre after the great 1835 fire. The album of engineering drawings covers railroad bridges, a tunnel, and canal locks. A few drawings portray his work outside the city, including an 1834 plan for the base of a proposed Washington Monument in the District of Columbia. Many of the schemes follow a Greek Revival style.

Figure 82. Unidentified brownstone, New York City. Elevation. Ink and watercolor drawing by Calvin Pollard, ca. 1840. (Neg. no. 64105)

Arrangement and access: Drawings are filed by a Society-assigned number that reflects a general grouping by building type. A card index provides access by building type to a short description of each drawing.
Provenance: Gifts from Samuel V. Hoffman in 1912 and 1927 and from E. H. Sauer in 1913.
References: Most of the drawings are described in George S. Koyl, editor, *American Architectural Drawings… to 1917* (Philadelphia: American Institute of Architects Philadelphia Chapter, 1969).
Related: Pollard's pocket diaries (1841–1842) and a contract for remodeling Castle Garden are in the Manuscript Department. A watercolor rendering by Pollard of the Henry Remsen residence is in the Department of Paintings, Sculpture, and Decorative Arts .
At other institutions: The Avery Architectural and Fine Arts Library at Columbia University also has drawings by Pollard.

Figure 83. *The Honble. John Hancock Esqr.* State I. Mezzotint with touches of watercolor by Joseph Hiller, Sr., after an oil painting by John Singleton Copley, ca. 1776. (Neg. no. 41408)

Wealthy merchant John Hancock (1736/37-1793) had his portrait painted by John Singleton Copley in Boston, Massachusetts, in the early 1770s. The painting captured Hancock's handsome features and confidence. At least two printmakers, including Hiller (1748-1814), copied the painting in the mid-1770s to distribute an image of this popular American independence movement leader.

52. PORTRAIT FILE

ca. 1500–present, bulk 1800–1930.
ca. 45,000 prints and photographs.

The Society has assembled an extensive file of portraits. Formats and media vary widely from ordinary black-and-white engravings based on paintings to rare hand-colored mezzotints (Figure 83) and from posed professional studio photographs to informal snapshots. Likenesses of American men who achieved national fame before 1930 predominate. There are also numerous images of prominent New Yorkers, theatrical personalities, and eminent Europeans who figure in United States history. The file contains as well views of birthplaces, statues, tombs, and association items. There are many portraits of United States presidents through Franklin D. Roosevelt and of the poet Walt Whitman and other celebrities of the 1800s. People or organizations whose papers or artwork are at the Society also tend to be well-represented, including statesman Albert Gallatin, sculptor John Rogers, the Seventh Regiment of the New York National Guard, hotel association members, and the Salmagundi Club. Several large collections are dispersed in the file by sitters' surnames: thousands of portraits culled chiefly from illustrated books and donated by Robert Fridenberg; and ca. 250 prints by Albert and Max Rosenthal of celebrated historical figures. Special sets that have been kept together include photographs of more than 3,000 original silhouettes cut by Auguste Edouart during his visit to the United States from 1839 to 1849; ca. 100 etchings and engravings made by Jacques Reich between 1884 and 1923; and hundreds of photographs taken by the Pach Brothers from 1867-1947.

The theatrical portraits feature actors and actresses who performed on New York stages (Figure 84) and show many dressed for their famous roles. Gertrude and Raphael Weed contributed some 2,000 well-captioned photographs of players popular in the 1800s. Other generous donors of theatrical material include Edmund B. Child, Robert Goelet, and Harold Seton, who also gave more than 100 photographs of people who attended the famous Vanderbilt costume ball in 1883. Of special interest are the many likenesses of Jenny Lind donated by Leonidas Westervelt. Concert singer Emma Thursby and her associates are also heavily represented.

Arrangement and access: Images are filed alphabetically by sitters' surnames, with separate sections for small theatrical portraits, costume balls, group portraits, unidentified people, Edouart silhouette photographs, and Reich prints. There are finding aids for the Edouart photographs, Pach Brothers photographs, Reich prints, Rosenthal prints, and Weed Collection photographs. Some access to portrait creators and such subjects as weddings is available through the Negative File index.
Related: Many other collections feature portraits and can be located through the index to this guide. The Department of Paintings, Sculpture, and Decorative Arts also has numerous portraits. The Manuscript Department often has the family papers of people heavily represented in the file.

Figure 84. Lillian Russell. Photograph by Napoleon Sarony, copyright 1891. (Neg. no. 7260)

Singing and acting star Lillian Russell (1861–1922) charmed audiences with her pleasant voice and striking beauty. Photographer Napoleon Sarony posed Russell with a sedan chair, in costume for her title role in *The Grand Duchess* at the Casino Theatre in New York City.

53. GEORGE B. POST ARCHITECTURAL RECORD COLLECTION

ca. 1860-1950; bulk 1880-1910.

ca. 8,600 architectural drawings, ink on linen and blueprints; ca. 200 watercolor renderings, ink drawings, and pencil sketches; 75 packages of specifications; 5 albums of photographs; 1,000 separate photographs; 2 clipping scrapbooks (1882-1903); 5 letterpress books (1867-1884); ca. 1,700 incoming letters (1872-1875); 1 ledger and 1 journal of Gambrill & Post (1864-1867); ca. 60 financial ledgers and journals (1868-1951); 2 volumes of personnel employment records (1881-1918); 1 package of publications by firm members.

George Browne Post (1837-1913) completed a degree in civil engineering and worked as a draftsman for Richard Morris Hunt before opening an architectural office in New York in 1860 with Charles D. Gambrill. By 1868, Post had his own firm, which specialized in commercial architecture. His structural design skills and efficient, economical plans won him many honors, but only a handful of the more than 400 projects he undertook in New York City, Cleveland, Buffalo, and elsewhere have survived the urban rebuilding of recent decades. Post is noted today for his tall arcaded buildings, which are among the first skyscrapers, and for his role in developing the modern office building. He also collaborated on lavish mansions for such clients as Cornelius Vanderbilt and Collis P. Huntington (Figure 85).

The Society's collection contains most of the surviving records of Gambrill & Post (1860-1867), Geo. B. Post (1868-1905), and Geo. B. Post & Sons (founded 1905). Projects before 1890—for example, the Equitable Life Assurance (Figure 86) and Western Union buildings in New York City—are covered primarily through financial journals, correspondence, photographs, and some 50 sketches and watercolor renderings by Post and by Edward A. Sargeant. For later projects, more documentation is usually available, from competition entries and developmental studies to working drawings, construction progress photographs, specifications, business ledgers, and publicity clippings. Sets of drawings document some 30 large hotels; 20 office buildings, including the St. Paul Building, New York; 20 banks and exchanges, including the New York Produce Exchange and the New York Stock Exchange; 10 apartment buildings and housing developments; 5 schools and colleges, including the College of the City of New York; the Wisconsin State Capitol; and more than 50 residences, many designed by William S. Post for relatives and neighbors in Bernardsville, New Jersey. Late commissions include an omnibus garage and the Netherlands Pavilion at the 1939-1940 New York World's Fair.

Arrangement and access: Material is filed by format. Working drawings are in numbered sets according to project name; most renderings, competition entries, and sketches are alphabetical by project name; financial volumes are grouped by type (ledger, journal, cash book, staff pay record) and date; individual photographs are

grouped by project name. Lisa Mausolf's thesis provides an alphabetical listing and chronological index to all of Post's known projects and indicates for which buildings the Society has study, presentation, and working drawings. Separate card indexes provide access by project name for drawings and for photographs in two of the albums.
Provenance: Gift from Post's grandson, Edward E. Post, in 1956, with additions in 1972 and 1978.
References: Lisa B. Mausolf, "A Catalog of the Work of George B. Post, Architect" (Master's thesis, Columbia University, 1983). Winston Weisman, "The Commercial Architecture of George B. Post," *Journal of the Society of Architectural Historians* 31 (Oct. 1972): 176-203.

Figure 86. Equitable Life Assurance Society Building, New York City. Watercolor by George B. Post, ca. 1868. (Neg. 48485)

Figure 85. Study for corbel in the library of residence for Collis P. Huntington, New York City. Pen and ink drawing by the George B. Post firm, 1892. (Neg. no. 57661)

George Post's large architectural firm handled a wide range of commissions. The drawing above shows an elaborate library corbel (bracket) for a residence designed in mid-Manhattan for Collis P. Huntington, a wealthy railroad, mining, and shipping magnate. The rendering on the left is a competition proposal for the Equitable Life Assurance Society's first home office. Equitable rejected this design, but then hired Post as an associate architect to re-engineer the winning scheme, which was similar in appearance, and make it affordable to build. The eight-story structure, at 120 Broadway in lower Manhattan, was among New York's first tall buildings and is sometimes called the city's first skyscraper. Its early use of passenger elevators meant that additional floors and rental space were possible. Post believed in tall buildings. When skeptics warned that the upper stories would be unrentable, Post leased space for his own firm. He later declined to move when the building proved to be an immediate success. The building burned in 1912 (see Figure 94).

Figure 87. *Adirondack Mountains, St. Huberts, Keene Heights.* Postcard, color photomechanical print by Hugh C. Leighton Co., Portland, Maine, and Frankfort am Main, Germany, mailed January 30, 1907. (Neg. no. 64695)

In this typical vacation postcard, golfers appear in front of a resort hotel. The summer scene, however, contrasts with the winter mailing date from Saranac Lake, New York.

54. POSTCARD FILE
ca. 1890–present, bulk 1900–1940.
ca. 50,000 postcards, including color lithographs, photomechanical prints, and photographic prints.

Mailable cards were introduced in the United States in the 1870s, chiefly for advertisements and business notices. Pictorial cards issued for the 1893 Columbian Exposition popularized view cards. The 1898 reduction in postcard postage, from two cents to a penny, triggered a flood of card production. Millions of cards were mailed and collected annually through World War I. The Society's file features unused view cards from that golden postcard era through the 1930s. Most of the cards record attractive urban life as shown in courthouses and libraries, impressive office buildings, and spacious parks. Numerous souvenir cards depict such popular tourist spots as the Brooklyn Bridge and Niagara Falls or vacation resorts by the sea and in the mountains (Figure 87). The Society actively acquires less common New York State views, such as actual photographs on postcard stock that document towns or events too small to appear in formal publications. Postcards commissioned by restaurants and hotels also often provide valuable visual documentation of sites not otherwise represented in the collections. New York City views predominate (11,000 cards); followed by the rest of New York State (13,000 cards); all other areas of the United States (22,000 cards); and Canada, Bermuda, and the Caribbean (1,600 cards). The remaining cards depict ships, trains, political and other portraits, and comic scenes. Novelty cards include views in which windows or street lamps appear to be lit when the cards are held against a strong light. Many major postcard publishers are represented, among them the Detroit Publishing Company. Approximately 10,000 cards came from the stock file of the Brooklyn-based Albertype Company, run by the Wittemann family.

Arrangement and access: View postcards are filed geographically by country, state, and city; large cities are subdivided by building types, street names, and subjects. The "Other" category includes comic cards, portraits, ships, and greeting cards. The "Unusual" category has novelty cards. Staff can be consulted for choice of categories.
Related: Fold-out souvenir viewbooks are in the Geographic File. Photocopies of the New York City "Hotels" and "Restaurants" postcards are interfiled in the Geographic File for ready reference.

Figure 88. *Harper's January.* Magazine poster, color lithograph from drawing by Edward Penfield, published by Harper and Brothers, 1895. (Neg. no. 70807)

In April 1893, Harper and Brothers introduced a new form of advertising to New York: colorful placards, approximately 18 × 13 in., with boldly outlined figures and few words. Artist Edward Penfield (1866–1925), head of the Harper's art department, designed the publisher's monthly magazine posters from April 1893 to July 1899. The poster shown here is in yellow, green, orange, and blue. The design depicts an attractive man and woman, each with a copy of the magazine; their heavy coats emphasize the time of year.

55. POSTER FILE
ca. 1790–present, bulk 1890–1945.
ca. 5,000 posters, including woodcuts, lithographs, and photomechanical prints.

The Poster File encompasses several types of notices designed to attract attention from a distance: theater playbills and circus posters, book and magazine placards, war posters, and political and cultural posters. The earliest items are the chiefly printed text playbills that provide a detailed record of performances in New York City from the 1790s to the 1890s by announcing the basic facts of theater name, play title, performing cast, and date. The livelier circus promotions include a rare multi-sheet woodcut from the mid-1800s. Early black-and-white advertisements for magicians, menageries, and human curiosities are followed by large color promotions for the Ringling Brothers and Barnum & Bailey circuses. There are also posters for agricultural fairs and for New York world's fairs.

A large group of placards advertises issues of *Black Cat, The Century, The Chap-book, Harper's* (Figure 88), *Lippincott's, Scribner's,* several bicycle magazines, books, and newspapers. They were produced during a brief American art poster craze, launched in the 1890s when New

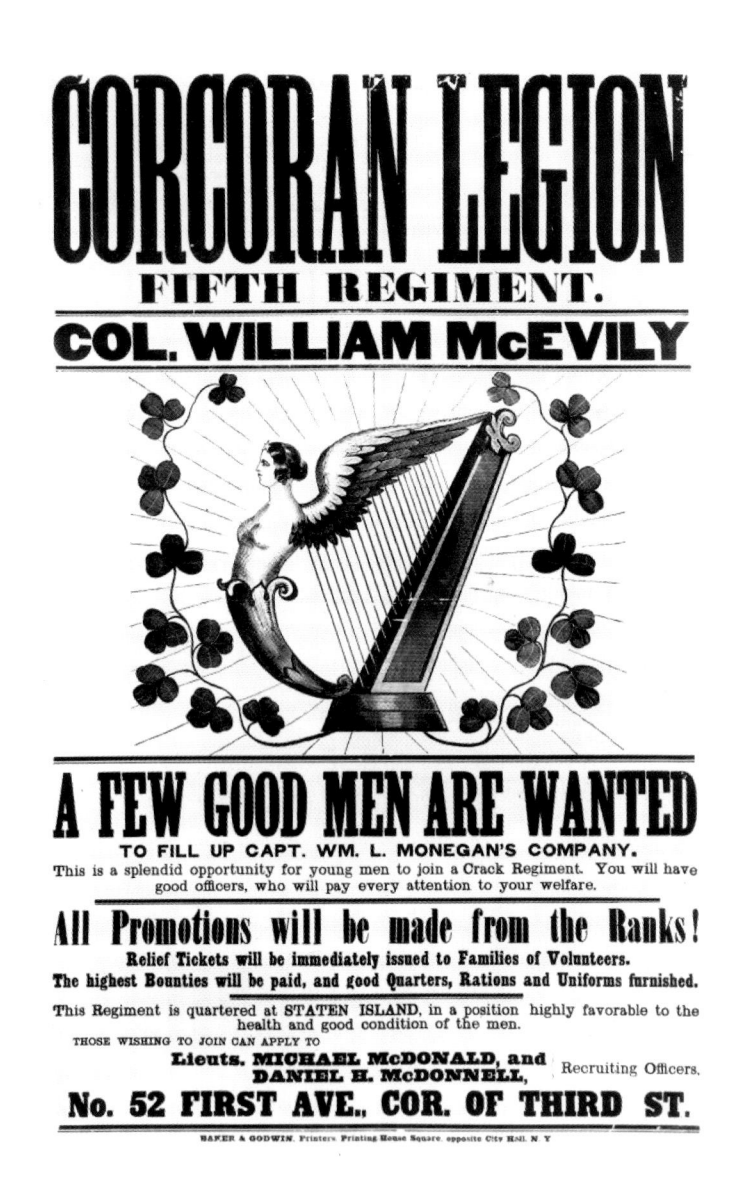

Figure 89. *Corcoran Legion, Fifth Regiment.* Recruiting poster by Baker & Godwin Printers, New York, ca. 1862. (Neg. no. 42687)

In the 1850s, more than one quarter of Manhattan's and Brooklyn's residents were Irish immigrants. The poster offers promotion from the ranks, relief tickets for families, good quarters and rations, and uniforms. Michael Corcoran, who emigrated from Ireland in 1849, became a Union general during the Civil War and began the Corcoran Legion in 1862.

York publishers hired Edward Penfield, Joseph J. Gould, and other illustrators to create striking graphics to sell their monthly magazines. The bold, clever images, inspired by French art styles and by the Arts and Crafts movement, became so collectible that publishers soon switched to monthly pictorial covers instead of posters.

Numerous examples of war posters are available, starting with Civil War and other recruiting announcements (Figure 89). Posters reached another artistic peak during World War I, when governments and organizations issued thousands of pictorial sheets to persuade citizens to enlist, buy bonds, conserve fuel, and otherwise support the war effort. The Society began collecting World War I posters when the United States entered the war in 1917 and has ca. 1,200 American issues, including Montgomery Flagg's famous "I Want You," as well as some hundred sheets from England, France, and Germany. There are also more than 500 American posters from World War II. The remainder of the file consists of about 100 political election posters and a few announcements for labor rallies and local exhibitions.

Arrangement and access: Posters are grouped by broad category: Book and Magazine; Circus; Fairs; General (including recruiting, war, and cultural); Politics; and Theater. They are subarranged by date, subject, or sponsor (e.g., a circus name). The Negative File catalog provides a ready reference to the most popular images under *Posters*.

Related: The Landauer Collection has most of the Society's advertising posters and numerous other posters. The Strobridge Collection has circus and theatrical posters. The Reading Room has extensive collections of playbills and broadsides.

56. VICTOR PREVOST PHOTOGRAPH COLLECTION
ca. 1854.
44 calotype negatives (10 ½ × 13 in.) and contact prints made ca. 1900 (11 × 14 in.).

French artist Victor Prevost (1820-1881) established himself as a painter in New York City, ca. 1850. During a visit to France in 1853, he mastered Gustave Le Gray's calotype (waxed paper negative) process and then worked as a professional photographer in Manhattan for several years. Despite admiration for his calotypes, Prevost could not earn a living with photography, and he turned to teaching drawing and physics in 1857. The artfully composed scenes at the Society are thought to be the earliest surviving photographic views of New York City and were apparently taken to illustrate a proposed book. They are prized as fine examples of the calotype process, which was rarely used in the United States. The images portray 23 sites from Battery Place and lower Broadway's commercial buildings (Figure 90) to the Crystal Palace exhibition, scattered buildings in upper Manhattan, and churches around East 28th Street, near Prevost's home. Some images are signed and dated 1854 in the negative. W.I. Scandlin researched and captioned the photographs, which were among a group of more than 100 Prevost negatives discovered in an attic in 1898.

Arrangement and access: The original negatives are filed by an assigned number that corresponds to the finding aid's alphabetical list of captions. Reference prints, made ca. 1900, are available as a unit. Copy negatives made from the reference prints are indexed in the Negative File catalog.

Provenance: Gift from Samuel V. Hoffman in 1906.

References: W.I. Scandlin, "Victor Prevost," *Photo Era* (Oct. 1901): 126-131. Thirteen images are reproduced in Mary Black, *Old New York in Early Photographs* (New York: Dover, 1976).

At other institutions: The International Museum of Photography at George Eastman House and the National Museum of American History Division of Photographic History each have ca. 50 Prevost calotypes of France, Central Park, and other topics. The New York Public Library has albums of Central Park views from the 1860s and 1870s.

Figure 90. Gori's marble working establishment, 897 Broadway, New York City. Calotype by Victor Prevost, ca. 1854. (Neg. no. 26140)

Ottaviano Gori lived above his marble cutting workshop on Broadway between 19th and 20th Streets in lower Manhattan. The sculpture atop the building advertises his wares along with the many statues, busts, and monuments visible behind the windows and next to the bluestone sidewalk.

57. PRINTING PLATE FILE

ca. 1770–ca. 1950.
ca. 750 items: 170 engraving plates, 420 woodblocks, 150 photomechanical and other plates, and 9 lithographic stones.

The file contains examples from the late-1700s to the mid-1900s of common and unusual printing processes, including copper engravings and etchings, wood engravings, photomechanical plates, woodblocks, and etched lithographs. New Yorkers created most of the plates, blocks, and stones, primarily for such commercial assignments as calling cards, book and periodical illustrations, city views, and cartoons. This material is valued for the information it provides about printing techniques. For some images, the Society also owns original drawings and printed impressions, which provide additional insight into print production. In other cases, a plate may be important because it represents the only surviving copy of an image. The earliest works are copperplates: Henry Dawkins' engraving for Sir William Johnson's 1770 Indian testimonial, New York area maps published in the *Atlantic Neptune,* a medallion portrait of George Washington engraved by B.L. Prevost, and the 1796 view of New York from Long Island drawn and etched by Charles Balthazar Julien Févret de Saint-Mémin. A pair of copperplates engraved by William James Bennett after Nicolino Calyo depicts the disastrous 1835 New York City fire. Another large plate engraved by Sigismond Himely after John W. Hill shows New York as an active seaport in 1852. Modern plates include copper etchings by local artist Gottlob Briem and photomechanical book illustrations. Of special interest among the woodblocks are ca. 375 small illustrations by the prolific Alexander Anderson, who is considered the father of American wood engraving. There are also several uncut blocks with caricatures by Thomas Worth, who produced similar images for Currier & Ives. The lithographic stones include three etched outline illustrations made by popular artist F.O.C. Darley, ca. 1850, for novels by James F. Cooper.

Arrangement and access: Most items are labeled by title or printer. Consult staff for access.
Related: Prints made from many of the plates and blocks are available in other files. The Bookplate File contains several bookplate printing plates. The Wright Collection includes photomechanical printing equipment. The Department of Paintings, Sculpture, and Decorative Arts has four copper engraving plates for John J. Audubon's *The Birds of America.* The Reading Room has numerous printing plates for children's book illustrations from the McLaughlin Brothers firm.

Figure 91. View of Fort George, New York, from the west. Hand-colored mezzotint attributed to William Burgis, New York, 1730–1731. (Neg. no. 15897)

Fort George stood on the site of Manhattan's U.S. Custom House near Bowling Green from ca. 1626 to 1790. Artist William Burgis, who worked in the American colonies from 1718 until after 1731, drew the British colors flying over the fort and a man-of-war firing a broadside. Since the Society bought this previously unknown American print in 1949, no other impressions have been discovered.

58. PRINTMAKER FILE
ca. 1730–present, bulk 1800–1860.
ca. 500 prints: aquatints, engravings, etchings, lithographs, and woodcuts.

The Printmaker File contains prints which are likely to be known or studied because of their creators or because of their significance in the history of American printmaking. Most of the images depict areas of New York City and New York State before the Civil War. Among the beautiful scenic sets are lithographs for Jacques Milbert's *Itinéraire Pittoresque du Fleuve Hudson...* and *A Series of Picturesque Views in North America;* John Hill's hand-colored aquatints for Joshua Shaw's *Picturesque Views of American Scenery* and for William G. Wall's *Hudson River Portfolio;* William J. Bennett's aquatints for *Megarey's Street Views in the City of New-York* (Introduction, Figure 18) and many of his fine folio views of American cities; Anthony Imbert's lithographs of public buildings in New York from drawings by Alexander J. Davis; and Henry Hoff's color lithographs for *Views of New York*. Rare individual prints include the unique *View of Fort George,* attributed to William Burgis and the first mezzotint of New York (Figure 91). In addition to topographic views, there are such early American treasures as Paul Revere's *Boston Massacre;* Alexander Anderson's large male anatomical figure; numerous engravings by the Mavericks; Asher B. Durand's nude *Ariadne;* and double elephant folio engravings by Robert Havell, Jr., for John J. Audubon's *The Birds of America.* Two specimen sheets attributed to Arthur J. Stansbury are thought to be the first lithographs printed in New York. There are also sets of prints issued by the American Art Union, including James D. Smillie's engravings of Thomas Cole's *Voyage of Life,* and by the Society of Iconophiles. The Currier & Ives material includes genre scenes and religious scenes.

Arrangement and access: Prints are filed by printmakers' names. Entries in the Artists and Engravers Index and in the Printers and Publishers Index identify the printmakers and briefly describe the prints.
References: Works by John Hill are described in Richard J. Koke, *A Checklist of the American Engravings of John Hill…* (New York: The Society, 1961). Summaries of the collection's strengths appear in Wendy Shadwell, "Prized Prints: Rare American Prints Before 1860 in the Collection of The New-York Historical Society," *Imprint 11* (Spring 1986): 1-27 and in Larry E. Sullivan, "The Print Collection of The New-York Historical Society," *Imprint 6* (Autumn 1981): 20-24.
Related: Many rare prints are also in the Caricature, Geographic, Portrait, and Subject files and in special collections such as the Olds Collection. The Department of Paintings, Sculpture, and Decorative Arts has original drawings and paintings by many of the artists and printmakers represented in this file. The Manuscript Department has the papers of Alexander Anderson, John Hill, and Samuel Maverick and the records of the American Art Union.

59. JACOB A. RIIS REFERENCE PHOTOGRAPH COLLECTION
ca. 1872–ca. 1900, bulk 1890–1900, printed 1950.
ca. 225 modern photographic prints (8 × 10 in.).

Social reformer Jacob August Riis (1849–1914) immigrated to the United States in 1870 and lived in poverty for several years before becoming a newspaper police reporter on Manhattan's Lower East Side. In the 1880s, he began his effective crusade to improve immigrants' living conditions through tenement house law reform and programs for children. Riis turned to photography in 1887 as a powerful tool to persuade people that the slum horrors were real. At first, he relied on Richard H. Lawrence and other amateur camera club members to obtain images. Soon he was taking his own photographs and also borrowing earlier views from Board of Health files and newspaper photographers. Riis shocked his lantern slide show audiences with views of Chinese, Greek, Italian, and Jewish immigrants' quarters, sweatshops, ragpickers, gangs, police station lodging houses, and prisons. He also showed them solutions available through street cleaning, playgrounds, a Children's Aid Society farm, and the transformation of the Mulberry Bend slum into an urban park. The Society's prints represent about half the original images at the Museum of the City of New York, including the best known ones and all the topics mentioned above.

Arrangement and access: Prints are filed by Riis number. The finding aid is a checklist of titles by Riis number. Subject access is available by consulting Robert J. Doherty, *The Complete Photographic Work of Jacob A. Riis* (New York: Macmillan, 1981), in which the photographs are listed in topical categories with references to Riis numbers.
Provenance: Purchase in ca. 1950 from Alexander Alland, who made the prints from the original negatives now at the Museum of the City of New York.
Related: Similar slum images are in the Richard H. Lawrence Collection. The Manuscript Department has two manuscript articles by Riis.
At other institutions: The Museum of the City of New York has the major Riis photograph collection, with more than 400 glass negatives and 150 lantern slides. The Library of Congress, Manuscript Division, has Riis' papers and scrapbooks.

60. JOSEPH SCANLON COLLECTION OF STEAMBOAT PHOTOGRAPHS
ca. 1830-1960.
ca. 5,000 photographic prints (most 4 × 5 in.), ca. 600 film negatives (most 2¼ × 4¼ in.), and a few glass negatives. Accompanied by 5 boxes of steamboat information cards, 6 boxes of research notes, and some correspondence.

Joseph Scanlon (died 1968?) compiled an extensive pictorial reference file documenting New England, New York, and Middle Atlantic region steamboats (half of the material); ferryboats; Atlantic coastal steamers; and trans-Atlantic steamers, including some ocean liners. Broadside views of vessels underway predominate, although some boats are shown under construction, in a harbor setting, or as wrecks. Most images are photographic copies of photographs, drawings, paintings, and plans made during the 1800s and early 1900s, which Scanlon acquired from the Mariners' Museum, the Steamship Historical Society of America, The New-York Historical Society, and other sources. Prints and negatives marked "Scanlon Collection" appear to have been taken by Scanlon himself of New York City area steamers and ferries during the 1930s to 1950s. The prints are often captioned only by boat name and picture source, and the card information file contains such notes as where and when a steamer was built, tonnage, type of engine, and ownership history.

Arrangement and access: Photographs are filed by type of vessel (Steamboats, Ferryboats, Coastwise Steamers, and Trans-Atlantic Steamers), then alphabetically by vessel name, except for trans-Atlantic steamers, which are filed by line name. The steamboat information card file is in one alphabet by vessel name. This information file includes descriptions of some vessels for which Scanlon did not have photographs. The finding aid summarizes the collection's scope and the filing categories.
Provenance: Gift from Joseph Scanlon in 1956 and bequest in 1968.
Related: Steamboat material is also in the LeBoeuf Collection, the Murdock Collection, and the Subject File.
Restrictions: Permission is required to reproduce images credited to other institutions.

Figure 92. Rhealee Hat Shop, 408 Fifth Avenue, New York City. Photograph by Joseph W. Molitor, 1940s. (Neg. no. 70802)

61. S.S. SILVER & COMPANY COLLECTION OF STORE DISPLAY PHOTOGRAPHS

1920s–1950s, bulk 1940s–1950s.
49 albums (more than 750 black-and-white and color photographic prints) and ca. 50 loose prints. Accompanied by 2 publicity scrapbooks, several floor design plans, 1 company manual (1946), and 1 folder of correspondence with clients.

The Brooklyn-based S.S. Silver & Company designed floor display installations (Figure 92) for such New York City stores as Arnold Constable, Bergdorf Goodman, Georg Jensen, and the Ideal Novelty & Toy Company. Department stores are heavily represented, particularly Saks Fifth Avenue in several cities and Woolf Brothers in Kansas City, Missouri. There are also a few office and residential interiors, including the home of the firm's founder, Sol S. Silver. Joseph W. Molitor of New York City took many of the architectural photographs on which credit lines are visible. Caption information is sparse.

Arrangement and access: Most photographs are in albums compiled by the Silver Company. The finding aid is the company's own checklist of albums, which names the store illustrated and the quantity of photographs.
Provenance: Gift from Bertram S. Silver in 1982.
Restrictions: The photographer's permission may be necessary to reproduce photographs credited to commercial photographers.

Figure 93. Pinkney garden pump, north of W. 139th Street, east of Seventh Avenue, New York City. Glass negative by James Reuel Smith, April 21, 1898. (Neg. no. 63813-H-16)

A detail from a larger view is reproduced here to emphasize the features of the pump set over a well in a flower garden at the rear of the Pinkney House in upper Manhattan. In his book, James Reuel Smith described the grounds, which extended from 139th to 141st Street, as part of the Watt estate. During his visit, he saw a long stable with 35 horses and ponies, including a Shetland pony born that morning. He also learned that another well on the place had been filled up only two weeks earlier because it began to smell bad.

62. JAMES REUEL SMITH SPRINGS AND WELLS PHOTOGRAPH COLLECTION
ca. 1900.
ca. 350 photographic prints and ca. 280 glass negatives (most 4 × 5 in.).

An inherited income enabled James Reuel Smith (1852–1935) to pursue his own interests. His contributions to amateur photography included several articles in the *American Annual of Photography* that offer tips for solving such problems as photographing sunlit interiors. The Society's collection features his interest in New York City springs. From 1897 to 1901, Smith bicycled around Manhattan and the Bronx to track down the last outdoor springs and wells. He photographed and described in detail some 100 sites, all of which he found north of 61st Street. His images document not only a vanishing water supply source but a variety of settings: neglected basins in rapidly urbanizing residential areas, hand pumps (Figure 93), elaborate dome-covered wells in estate gardens, and idyllic park sites. Children pose in numerous scenes. There are also photographs of a few wells in Brooklyn, street scenes, and several portraits of Smith.

Arrangement and access: One group of prints is mounted on card stock and filed geographically by borough and street name. Portraits of Smith and a group of unmounted prints (including the same views as the mounted set) and miscellaneous mounted prints are in separate folders. Most prints are captioned and keyed to negative numbers. Captions on negative jackets are keyed to illustration numbers in Smith's book. The Negative File catalog indexes neighborhoods and basic subjects, but not individual streets.
Provenance: Bequest from the photographer in 1937.
References: James R. Smith, *Springs and Wells of Manhattan and the Bronx, New York City, at the End of the Nineteenth Century, with 154 Illustrations* (New York: Printed for The New-York Historical Society, 1938).
Related: Smith's extensive notes and clippings about springs are in the Reading Room.

Figure 94. Equitable Building fire, New York City. Glass negative by Frederick H. Smyth, 1912. (Neg. no. 61055-106280)

The Equitable Life Assurance Society's home office at 120 Broadway burned down in 1912. Architect George Post had helped to design the structure in 1868–1870 (see Figure 86). New developers erected a dense 40-story office building on the site in 1912–1915, but kept the name of the earlier structure.

63. FREDERICK H. SMYTH COLLECTION OF FIRE PHOTOGRAPHS

ca. 1900–1920.
2 albums (ca. 375 photographic prints);
ca. 375 negatives and a few transparencies, most glass and a few film (6½ × 8½ in. and smaller, most 5 × 7 in.).

Frederick Hugh Smyth (1878–1949) made a hobby of taking and collecting photographs of New York City fires. In addition to such famous disasters as the 1911 Triangle Shirtwaist Company fire and the 1912 Equitable Building fire (Figure 94), his collection depicts the transition from horse-drawn to motorized equipment. A horseshoeing wagon, fireboats, inspection of new fire apparatus, portraits of Fire Department officials, and training exercises fill one album. The other album contains numerous fire scenes and ruins in Manhattan, the Bronx, and Queens.

Arrangement and access: The well-captioned album prints are keyed to negative numbers. (The albums are housed in the Album File.) Negatives are indexed by subject in the Negative File catalog, with a comprehensive listing under "Smyth."
Provenance: Gift from Robert E. Logan in 1958.
Related: The Geographic File has a large category of Bronx and Manhattan fires and fire companies. The Department of Paintings, Sculpture, and Decorative Arts has extensive collections of fire-related material, including fire buckets, hats, and medals.

64. JOHN B. SNOOK ARCHITECTURAL RECORD COLLECTION

ca. 1840-1950, bulk ca. 1870-ca. 1900.
ca. 2,500 architectural drawings, chiefly working drawings in ink, including some color elevations, and also several blueprints; 6 contract books (1843-1897), 7 ledgers (1845-1904), 7 account books (1860-1893), 10 receipt and expenditure ledgers (1865-1888), and 6 day books (1887-1910). Accompanied by a 1-volume drawing index.

The largely self-taught architect John Butler Snook (1815-1901) was a partner in several New York City firms during his long career: Trench & Snook, with partner Joseph Trench (1843-1857); John B. Snook (1857-1887); John B. Snook & Sons (1887-1901). His sons continued after 1901 as John B. Snook Sons. The Society has the only known body of Snook's work, which represents some 200 projects. The collection contains material for his two best-known commissions: the first Grand Central Depot, built for the Vanderbilt family, and the first elaborate department store, built for Alexander T. Stewart on Broadway (Figure 95). The drawings and financial records are also valuable for the information they provide about cast-iron structures and tenement housing. The majority of the designs are working drawings for office buildings, mercantile establishments, cold storage warehouses, power plants, tenements and private houses, stables, and a Hebrew Orphan Asy-

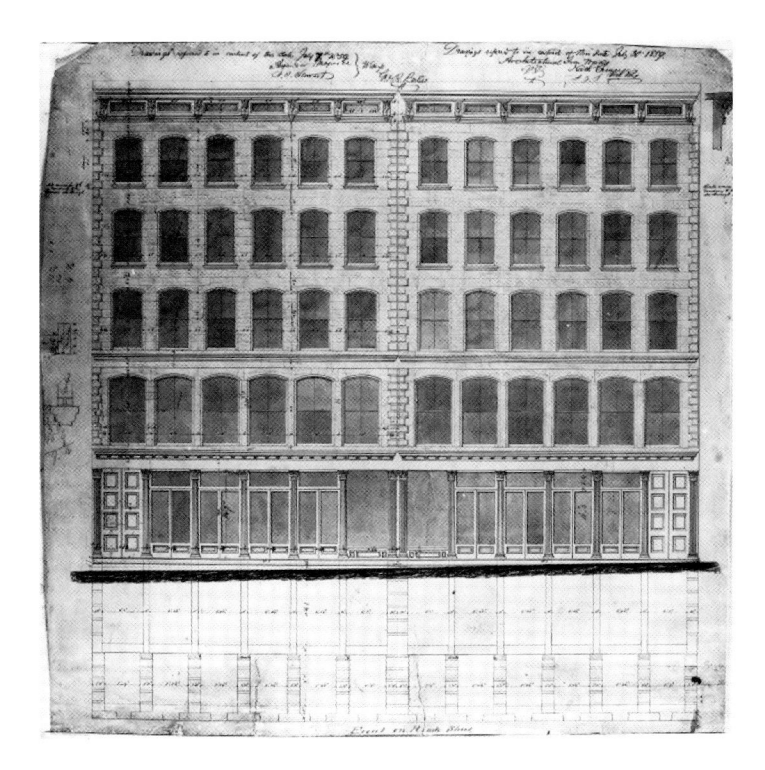

Figure 95. A.T. Stewart Store, New York City. John B. Snook, architect. Ink drawing, 1859. (Neg. no. 52491)

Dry goods merchant A.T. Stewart commissioned a lavish store from architect John B. Snook. Low markups and set prices on many kinds of goods attracted customers to the "Marble Palace," which opened in 1846 on Broadway between Reade and Chambers Streets, near City Hall. This contract drawing of the Reade Street elevation, signed in 1859 by A.T. Stewart, Alexander Maxwell, and Geo. B. Butler, was probably for renovation work.

lum. Although a few projects are outside New York City, most are in lower Manhattan—for example, a set of about 30 plans, elevations, and sections for a tenement at 244-246 Mulberry Street built in 1885. Drawings are usually identified by street address and client.

Arrangement and access: Drawings are filed by building or project name. The finding aid is a checklist of projects; entries are arranged geographically with descriptions of building name or street address, date, type of building, total number of items, and number of plans, elevations, and sections. A card catalog indexes each project alphabetically by name or address. Bound volumes are filed by type of record and date, with a summary description in the card index.
Provenance: Gift from the estate of Thomas E. Snook, Jr., in 1953, with a later gift of Grand Central Depot reproduction blueprints from Hermann Blumenthal in 1968.
References: Mary Ann Smith, "The Commercial Architecture of John Butler Snook" (Ph.D. dissertation, Pennsylvania State University, 1974). Mary Ann Smith, "John Snook and the Design for A.T. Stewart's Store," *The New-York Historical Society Quarterly* 58 (Jan. 1974): 18-33.
Related: The Reading Room has some 50 volumes from Snook's architectural library.

Figure 96. *Carmichael's Camp, Bitter Creek.* Photograph attributed to Andrew J. Russell, 1868 or 1869. Albumen print stereograph, published by O.C. Smith, Brooklyn, N.Y., 1875-1878. (Neg. no. 65017)

The large camera in the foreground reminds viewers of the stamina required by early wet-plate photographers in the West. They had to transport fragile glass negatives through rugged terrain, then coat them with sticky emulsions and quickly develop them before the collodion dried. New Yorker Andrew J. Russell (1830-1902) took this stereograph at Bitter Creek, Wyoming, while documenting Union Pacific Railroad construction as it progressed west from Cheyenne and through the Rocky Mountains.

65. STEREOGRAPH FILE

ca. 1855-1960s, bulk 1860-1900.
More than 13,600 stereographs, most albumen and other photographic prints, some photomechanical lithoprints (most mounted on ca. 4 x 7 in. cards); also some tintypes and glass transparencies.
Accompanied by several stereograph viewers.

Stereographs are pairs of almost identical images presented side by side to create, when seen through a special viewing device, a single, lifelike image with three-dimensional depth. First produced ca. 1850, they continue to be made in various media. In their heyday, from 1860 to 1920, millions of card-format stereographs were sold. City and town views, landscapes, wars, disasters, fairs, and staged comic dramas are the most common subjects. The bulk of the Society's file depicts New York City (2,600 cards), New York State (2,000 cards), other United States locales (4,200 cards), and the Civil War (1,200 cards). Views of the Brooklyn Bridge, Central Park, and Niagara Falls are particularly numerous, in keeping with the popularity of these sites. Many of the stereographs came from the collection of pharmacist George T. Bagoe (1886?-1948), who specialized in early New York views, Civil War scenes, Western exploration survey and railroad series, and stereographs in which the photographer's equipment is evident (Figure 96).

The file contains the majority of the Society's photographic coverage for the 1850s to 1870s, including examples of Anthony's *Instantaneous Views,* which captured people and carriages in motion at a time when most photographs offered empty streets because long exposure times erased anything that moved. Relatively few images in the file date later than 1900. A souvenir stereograph set portrays the 1939 World's Fair, and snapshots by amateur Alfred C. Loonan, some in color, depict Manhattan sites in the 1950s and 1960s. Views of foreign countries (1,200 cards) include color lithoprints distributed as free premiums by Quaker Oats. Among the items of special interest for the history of photography is a rare set of Central Park landscapes made by banker Frederick F. Thompson for the Amateur Photographic Exchange Club, ca. 1861 (Introduction, Figure 20). Other rare views include hand-tinted glass transparencies by the Langenheim Brothers (some of the first stereographs produced in the United States), a few tintypes, and a set of stereographs used to advertise a model house in St. Johnsbury, Vermont. Well-represented commercial photographers and publishers include: E. & H.T. Anthony, the Bierstadts, John Carbutt, F. Jay Haynes, William H. Jackson, Keystone View Company, Kilburn Brothers, Eadweard Muybridge, Andrew J. Russell, John P. Soule, Underwood & Underwood, and Carleton E. Watkins.

Arrangement and access: The file has two main sections—Geographic and Subject. The Geographic section is subdivided to the country, state, or city level, according to the quantity of cards for any one area. Large sections, for example "Manhattan," are subdivided into such specific categories as "Bridges—Brooklyn—Under construction." The Subject section includes Automobiles, Civil War, Comics, Disasters, Portraits, Railroads, Spanish-American War, and Sports, among other categories. The finding aid is a 29-page list of all file categories, with copies of 140 stereographs showing photographers at work and with references to unusual photographic processes and to some of the major photographers.

References: The Bagoe and Society collections are described in Lorraine Dexter, "American Collections of Stereoscopic Photographs," *Eye to Eye* 5 (June 1954): 3-23.

Related: Small-size stereo film and glass transparencies made after 1900 are in the Transparency File. One stereo daguerreotype is in the Cased Photograph File. An E. & H.T. Anthony salesman's stereograph stock book is in the Album File.

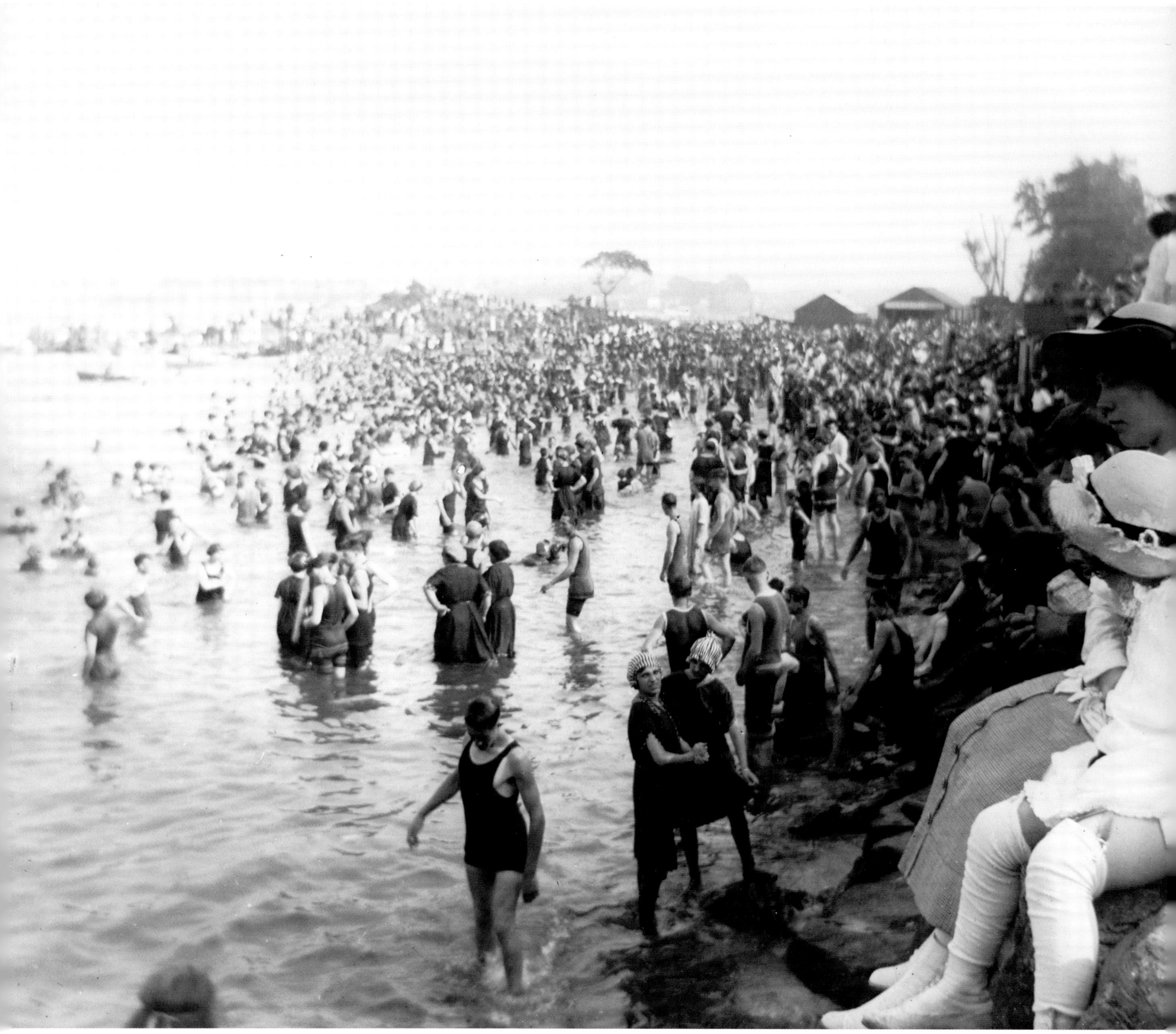

66. GEORGE E. STONEBRIDGE PHOTOGRAPH COLLECTION

ca. 1895-1915, bulk ca. 1900.

ca. 3,500 glass negatives (most 4 × 5 in.); ca. 1,100 corresponding prints; and several hundred transparencies and lantern slides. Accompanied by photographer's logbook.

Amateur photographer George Ehler Stonebridge preserved thousands of sharply focused scenes of outdoor family activities and local events, chiefly in the Bronx, ca. 1900. An active member of the Bronx Society of Arts and Sciences, Stonebridge was very proud of both the historic Bronx and the many urban developments he saw after moving to the borough in 1864. A sampling of his logbook categories indicates the subject coverage: Bronx parks; Croton strike; Navy Yard; Funeral of General Franz Sigel; Dewey Naval and Land Parade; Niagara; Jerome Park; May walk, 1898-1899; Cycle parade, 1897-1898; Wrecks; Fires; Sportsman's show; Hohenzollern-Stevens airship; Fordham; Portraits; Orchard Beach (Figure 97); City Island; Bronx clubs; Gas works (where Stone-bridge worked); New York Zoological Park (construction); Creedmoor (state militia camp); and Riverside Drive. There are also baseball teams in action; children throwing snowballs in Garrison, New York; and grim views of the *General Slocum* steamboat disaster victims.

Arrangement and access: Some prints are in the Geographic File. The remainder, often uncaptioned, are in a separate group. As prints are matched to corresponding negatives, each is filed by Stonebridge's negative number and specific subjects are indexed in the Negative File catalog. The lantern slides are in the Transparency File. The logbook provides access to negative numbers by subject categories such as those listed above.
Provenance: Gift from the photographer's widow, Mrs. George E. Stonebridge, in 1942.
Related: Some 20 rewards of merit issued to Stonebridge by the Morrisania School District are in the Certificate File. The Manuscript Department has a small group of Stonebridge family account books and miscellaneous letters. The Reading Room has his scrapbooks.

◀ Figure 97. Crowd of bathers, Orchard Beach, Bronx, New York. Glass negative by George E. Stonebridge, ca. 1910. (Neg. no. 63861-4488)

George Stonebridge frequently photographed the Orchard Beach area, which is part of Pelham Bay Park in the eastern Bronx, just north of City Island.

Figure 98. *A Giant Black Orang.* Barnum & Bailey circus poster. Chromolithograph by Strobridge Lithographing Company, Cincinnati and New York, ca. 1900. (Neg. no. 63983)

67. STROBRIDGE LITHOGRAPHING COMPANY POSTER COLLECTION
ca. 1885–ca. 1930.
ca. 1,000 prints (chiefly chromolithographs), ca. 1,500 photographs, and ca. 80 drawings.

The Cincinnati-based Strobridge Lithographing Company dated its founding to 1849 and closed in 1960. The firm began as a general commercial job printer but is best known for its color reproductions of oil paintings and for its lively, nationally distributed posters for circuses, plays, and other road show entertainments. The Society's collection features Strobridge's posters from ca. 1885 to 1930. Represented circus companies include Barnum & Bailey (Introduction, Figure 21 and Figure 98), Downie Brothers, Forepaugh & Sells, Ringling Brothers, Sells Brothers, and Buffalo Bill's Wild West show. The theatrical sheets depict individual actors, magicians, minstrel shows, operetta companies, motion pictures, and such perennial melodramas as "The White Slave" and "Only a Shop Girl." A file of 1,500 reference photographs documents posters produced from 1908 to 1928. There are also original sketches by noted illustrator Harry A. Ogden, who created many of the firm's circus designs in its New York office, and some finished drawings by an unidentified artist.

Arrangement and access: Posters are filed by category: Theatrical, Magicians, Minstrels, Portraits, Circus, and Miscellaneous. The finding aid is a card index with one entry per poster, for either the name of the play, performer, or circus company. The photographs of posters are filed chronologically and itemized in a checklist. The drawings are filed separately.

Provenance: Gift from James G. Strobridge in 1952 and 1956.

Related: A set of Strobridge calendars is in the Landauer Collection. A series of Strobridge lithographs commemorating Revolutionary War events and additional Ogden material are in the Subject File. Numerous circus and theatrical posters are also in the Landauer Collection and Poster File. The Manuscript Department has ca. 150 Strobridge bills and receipts, agreements with artists, and other items from 1854 to 1935.

At other institutions: The Cincinnati Historical Society has Strobridge account books, correspondence, and other records from 1867 to 1900.

Figure 99. *The Life and Age of Woman.* Woodcut published by Albert Alden, Barre, Massachusetts, ca. 1840. (Neg. no. 56785)

The "stages of woman's life from infancy to the brink of the grave" describe and depict what a woman experiences at ages 1, 12, 18, 30, 50, 75, and 90. Thirty is considered the prime of life: "A woman at this age in the strength of her mind, and at the height of her personal accomplishments, is ever sure, whether in the married or single state, to exert an influence that cannot fail to be salutary, if these are supported by religion." A companion piece covers the life and age of man.

68. SUBJECT FILE

ca. 1500-present, bulk 1800-1950.
ca. 30,000 prints and photographs.

The Subject File provides a wide variety of images of American history and life. Most of the prints and photographs depict wars and the maritime world, but sports, aviation, and many other topics are also represented. The early exploration and colonization of North America are shown chiefly through prints based on later artists' re-creations made in the 1800s and 1900s. Rare prints contemporary to a colonial event include three separate portrayals of four Iroquois sachems, known as the "Indian Kings," who visited the court of Queen Anne in 1710 (Introduction, Figure 16). Revolutionary War events appear in numerous patriotic engravings after works by historical painters John Trumbull and Alonzo Chappel. Prints of Charles M. Lefferts' series of meticulously drawn army uniforms are supplemented by sketches and clippings relating to historic military, civilian, and theatrical costumes collected by fellow illustrator Harry A. Ogden.

Prints portraying events during the War of 1812 dominate the years from 1789 to the eve of the Civil War with views of many naval engagements and such land actions as the Battle of the Thames. Mexican War battles are recorded in numerous lithographs published by Nathaniel Currier. Commodore Matthew C. Perry's 1853-1854 expedition to Japan is detailed in large contemporary color lithographs. Civilian life is documented in prints about coaching, crime and scandal, fashion, horse racing, and slavery. Among the more intriguing images is a moralistic woodcut showing the life and ages of woman (Figure 99). A rare Millerite banner, used by William Miller's followers to prove the world would end in 1843 or 1844, depicts a menagerie of biblical characters. There are also several scenes from *Uncle Tom's Cabin* and allegorical prints of Columbia and Liberty.

The Civil War is extensively documented in thousands of contemporary photographs and prints. Mathew Brady's *Album Gallery*, a set of small individually mounted photographs, and Harry P. Moore's photographs of freedmen on Edisto Island, South Carolina, deserve special mention as do the decoratively printed regimental rosters and numerous lithographs of battles and encampments by Currier & Ives, the Kelloggs, Kurz & Allison, and Edward Sachse. Spanish-American War coverage in photographs is also fairly extensive. There is relatively little for World War I besides Joseph Pennell's *War Work* lithographs. Most of the World War II images are government-issued photographs showing naval activities. Coverage of civilian life after the Civil War is relatively sparse. Material from the George T. Bagoe Collection and other sources features sports photographs, including fencing, wrestling, bicycling, and baseball; several cabinet card photographs portray circus performers; another group of cabinet cards documents live advertisements in Waterloo, Iowa (Figure 100). There are also numerous railroad photographs, Western Americana prints, decorative versions of the Declaration of Independence and similar documents, and a few European historical prints.

The importance of New York as a port city is reflected in the large selection of naval and maritime pictures, which features hundreds of prints from the Naval History Society Collection of naval engagements, individual ships, and portraits of officers. The Eugene H. Pool Collection con-

Figure 100. Woman wearing photographs to represent Mrs. G.M. Bowen's Banner Gallery. Cabinet card photograph by Mrs. G.M. Bowen, Waterloo, Iowa, 1889. (Neg no. 58051)

When Mrs. G.M. Bowen photographed participants in a merchant's fair, she included this young woman wearing photographs as a brooch, bracelets, and skirt decorations to represent Mrs. Bowen's own business. The fair has been identified as the Presbyterian Church Merchants' Carnival held May 21–22, 1889, in Waterloo, Iowa. This photograph is one of 17 cabinet cards, taken by Bowen and donated by George Bagoe, in which women are costumed with the goods of local businesses.

tributed nearly 50 prints related to Captain James Lawrence. Images of non-naval vessels include portraits of individual trans-oceanic, coastal, and inland steamboats; yachts; and harbor craft. The Hudson River Day Line is heavily represented in prints, photographs, steamboat blueprints, passenger schedules, handbills, and other business ephemera.

Arrangement and access: Most items are filed according to the historical time period depicted in the images, with separate sections for: Naval and Maritime history, Transportation, African Americans, Indians and the West, and Miscellaneous subjects. The finding aid is a checklist of filing categories.
References: Charles E. Baker, "The Eugene H. Pool Collection of Captain James Lawrence," *The New-York Historical Society Quarterly* 28 (Jan. 1944): 81-95. Hugh M. Flick, "The Harry A. Ogden Collection," *The New-York Historical Society Quarterly* 21 (Jan. 1937): 3-11.
Related: Images of local history events can usually be found in the Geographic File. For example, the *General Slocum* steamboat disaster, which happened in the East River, is filed with New York City.

146

69. SUBWAY CONSTRUCTION PHOTOGRAPH COLLECTION
ca. 1900-1940, bulk 1900-1920.
ca. 50,000 photographic prints (8 × 10 in.). Accompanied by route maps.

The New York City Board of Rapid Transit, the Public Service Commission, and their successors photographed construction of the subway (Figure 101), and its surface extensions in Manhattan, the Bronx, Brooklyn, and Queens. By systematically documenting the condition of buildings before construction began, they created an extensive survey of commercial and residential structures along subway routes and also provided glimpses of everyday street life (Figure 102). The Society's collection is strongest in views from 1900, when subway construction began, to 1920. The most heavily represented streets are Broadway and Lexington Avenue. Other photographs record underground tunneling, sewer reconstruction, pristine new stations, workmen, and such unexpected images as pool hall interiors. Most prints are identified by date, contract number, and location along a subway route. Despite the archive's size, the lack of some prints within assigned number ranges indicates that it is incomplete. A recent acquisition filled a gap of 80 views along Sixth Avenue in the 1930s.

Arrangement and access: Prints are filed in 38 sections that correspond to construction contracts. Within each contract, the sequence is chronological. The same street block may appear, therefore, in several places in the file—for example, before and during construction. A map of subway lines correlates current route names and geographic locations to contract segments. More than 700 images have been copied and indexed by specific subject and street address in the Negative File catalog.
Provenance: Gift from the Board of Transportation of New York City in 1950. A 1987 purchase added 80 prints.
Related: Additional subway images are in the Subject File. The Manuscript Department has Board of Trade and Transportation minutes and related papers, 1878-1914.
At other institutions: The New York City Transit Authority Archive has some photographs from the same series and chronological registers that describe each photograph.

◀ Figure 101. Vault light installation at City Hall loop, New York City.
Photograph, June 11, 1902. (Neg. no. 47759)

Figure 102. Lexington Avenue, view looking north from East 79th Street,
New York City. Photograph, November 1, 1911. (Neg. no. 59341)

In the 1902 picture, construction workers from Tucker & Vinton install vault lights near
City Hall (the two-story building at far left) in lower Manhattan. The bottom image,
one of an estimated 5,000 photographs that document buildings along the Lexington
Avenue subway route, shows such details of daily life as sidewalk chalk drawings
and a child looking at a "fancy groceries" store display of fruit and vegetables.

70. TRANSPARENCY FILE

ca. 1850–present, bulk ca. 1900–1960s.

ca. 7,400 items: 50 hand-painted slides; 3,000 lantern slides, chiefly black-and-white and some hand-colored (3¼ × 4 in.); 4,000 stereo slides, chiefly color film and some black-and-white glass (35mm); 200 color film slides (35mm); 150 color film slides (2¼ × 4¼ in.).

The file contains many types of transparencies—images intended to be viewed as light shines through them and often mounted for use in a projector. The earliest slides in the file are hand-painted glass discs with wooden frames designed for magic lantern entertainments. One set, made in the mid-1800s, illustrates scenes from *Uncle Tom's Cabin*. The largest portion of the file consists of the more common 3¼ × 4 in. lantern slide photographs, many of which resulted from the Society's sponsorship, from 1900 to 1950, of numerous illustrated lectures about New York and early American life. Some of these slides have become historic documents in their own right, such as original photographs taken to illustrate talks given in 1903 with then-contemporary views of such Manhattan neighborhoods as Chelsea, Greenwich Village, and Yorkville. Slides that reproduce textual documents, prints, songs, and museum objects are primarily of interest to students of historiography or educational methods. Well-represented photographers and manufacturers include Charles Beseler Co., Thomas J. Burton, George C. Dodd, and Edward Van Altena. In addition, there are lantern slides by skilled amateur photographers—for example, George E. Stonebridge's views of the Bronx.

Other sections of the file contain most of the Society's color and mid-1900s photographs of New York City. Robert M. Lester covered the 1947 Big Snow, New York art shows, and the United Nations area in almost 200 35mm transparencies made between 1947 and 1952. In the 1950s and 1960s, Carl Gerdau captured night scenes, street life, and structures in 150 color 2¼ × 2¼ in., glass-mounted film transparencies. Several thousand color stereo transparencies by Chester Burger document the 1964–1965 World's Fair, people in Central Park, and other New York City sights from 1952 to 1988. Daniel Coleman snapped family scenes and Manhattan's Upper West Side from 1954 to 1963. His small, captioned stereo slides number about 1,000 and are indexed on cards. A recent gift added close to 800 film stereo slides taken by G.L. Osmanson, from ca. 1959 to 1963, of ship passenger terminals, harbors, bridges, and Riverside Park.

Arrangement and access: Slides are filed by physical type or photographer and further subdivided by subject category or by an order set up by the photographer. Access to specific subjects is limited, although a card index lists some of the lantern slides and indicates which slides have corresponding negatives in the Negative File. Item-level checklists are available for the Coleman and Osmanson slides.

Related: Large (4 × 7 in.) glass transparency stereographs are in the Stereograph File. The Department of Rights and Reproductions has color 35mm slides and 4 × 5 in. and 8 × 10 in. copy transparencies of items in New-York Historical Society collections.

71. JOHN JUDSON TRAPPAN PHOTOGRAPH COLLECTION

ca. 1890–1905.
10 albums (462 photographic prints, black-and-white and cyanotype); ca. 290 loose and mounted prints; ca. 545 negatives (360 glass, most 4 × 5 in., and ca. 185 film). Accompanied by photocopy of photographer's logbook, 2 handwritten journals, and a few postcards, souvenir viewbooks, and bicycle ephemera.

Amateur photographer John Judson Trappan (died 1958) described his first photograph in a detailed logbook: "1890 Jan. 25, family group, parlor, 10:40 p.m., flash, stop no. 1, 5 × 8 inch, Sp. Ins. style Carbutt plate." Soon, he was filling small handmade albums with captioned cyanotypes and black-and-white prints from excursions on Long Island and north to Massachusetts. Trappan, as did many others, combined his camera enthusiasm with another popular pastime, bicycling. Two albums, "Berkshire Hills" and "A Coast Wise Trip A-Wheel," illustrate handwritten journals of bicycle trips. Other scenes depict his family in Brooklyn, co-workers at the Manhattan firm of Bruce & Cook, a church dinner, local outings, tourist landmarks in various cities, and the 1901 Pan-American Exposition in Buffalo. The last dated album is from his 1903 wedding trip to Philadelphia and Washington, D.C. Although Trappan and the family members who occasionally used his camera were not highly accomplished photographers, the albums together with the journals and logbook from 1890 to 1901 shed light on leisure activities and amateur photography at the turn of the century.

Arrangement and access: A checklist describes each album title and date, subject categories of loose prints, and accompanying ephemera.

Provenance: Gift from the photographer's daughter, Ruth Trappan, in 1984.

72. DORIS ULMANN PHOTOGRAPH COLLECTION

ca. 1910-1934.

ca. 3,000 photographic prints, most platinum (6 × 8 in.), and some photogravures.

Doris Ulmann (1882-1934) specialized in platinum portraits of prominent people and of rural Americans. A wealthy New Yorker, she studied with Clarence H. White in the 1910s and thereafter used a soft pictorial style for her carefully posed scenes. Her circle of acquaintances brought many well-known figures, particularly those in literary and theatrical fields, to her apartment-studio. Her work for portrait portfolios of the Columbia University medical faculty (1920), Johns Hopkins University medical faculty (1922), and American editors (1925) is in photogravure. After the mid-1920s, Ulmann continued to photograph famous individuals and created landscapes and still lifes, but she also wanted to make photographs of historical value. With folklorist John Jacob Niles, she sought out representative types of rural people to document disappearing ways of African-American life in coastal South Carolina and traditional Appalachian crafts in Kentucky and other states. Her photographs illustrate two books: *Roll, Jordan, Roll* by Julia Peterkin (1933) and *Handicrafts of the Southern Highlands* by Allan H. Eaton (1937).

Portraits constitute the bulk of the Society's holdings. Typical subjects include Sherwood Anderson, Calvin Coolidge, Esther Forbes (Figure 103), Martha Graham, Sinclair Lewis, and Edna St. Vincent Millay. There are also examples of some of her best-known African-American (Figure 104) and Appalachian photographs. Although many of the images in the Society's collection are unidentified, they are the largest known body of prints made by Ulmann herself and valuable records of how she intended her pictures to be presented. Some prints are signed. Early works bear her married name, Doris Jaeger.

Arrangement and access: The prints are filed by assigned numbers in broad categories: Identified Portraits (alphabetical by sitters' names); Unidentified Portraits (Children, Men, Women); Afro-Americans; Indians; Nuns and Monks; Still Lifes; and Landscapes. The Appalachian work is dispersed throughout these categories. The finding aid is a set of photocopies of the prints.
Provenance: Gift from the Doris Ulmann Foundation in 1954.
References: David Featherstone, *Doris Ulmann: American Portraits* (Albuquerque: University of New Mexico Press, 1985).
At other institutions: Ulmann's surviving glass negatives and albums with 10,000 reference prints made after her death are in the library at the University of Oregon. Several thousand prints, also made after her death, are at Berea College, Kentucky.

Figure 103. Esther Forbes. Photograph by Doris Ulmann, ca. 1930. (Neg. no. 64696)

Novelist and biographer Esther Forbes (1891-1967) gazes into the distance in this warm portrait. Forbes' first novel *O Genteel Lady!* achieved immediate success, and she won several honors, including the Pulitzer Prize for history (a biography of Paul Revere) and the 1944 Newbery Medal for *Johnny Tremain*.

Figure 104. African Americans entering a church, South Carolina. Photograph by Doris Ulmann, 1929-30. (Neg. no. 64181)

Doris Ulmann took this photograph as part of her work to document Gullah life for *Roll, Jordan, Roll*. The book has been called one of the first to merge the work of a writer and a photographer, but the 1933 trade edition had poorly reproduced illustrations. The later limited edition had high quality gravures, including this scene, and appeared shortly before Ulmann's death.

73. WINSTON WEISMAN COLLECTION OF ARCHITECTURAL PHOTOGRAPHS

ca. 1950–1975, depicting structures ca. 1850–1970.
ca. 3,500 photographic prints (8 × 10 in. and smaller) and ca. 3,800 film negatives (4 × 5 in. and smaller).
Accompanied by building reports, lectures, articles, maps, and a 5-box card file.

Architectural historian Winston R. Weisman compiled extensive pictorial documentation to support several areas of his research: cast-iron architecture, origins of the skyscraper, and commercial architecture in New York City, including the SoHo district, Rockefeller Center, and buildings by architect George B. Post. In addition to photographing extant buildings, he reproduced architectural drawings and book and magazine illustrations depicting structures in the 1800s and early 1900s. The collection's largest section documents cast-iron structures in the SoHo area of lower Manhattan in 1971 through notebooks of photographs and building reports created by Pennsylvania State University students under Weisman's direction (Figure 105). In the other section, mounted photographs depict commercial buildings in Manhattan (including many in SoHo and the Laing Stores), Chicago, Philadelphia, and a few other United States and foreign cities, chiefly from 1850 to 1950. Weisman captioned many of the photographs with information about architect and building construction date.

Arrangement and access: Photographs and data sheets in the SoHo notebooks are filed alphabetically by street name and are indexed by architect and building dates. Mounted prints are filed by city. The card file provides information about many buildings, arranged by date or by place.
Provenance: Gift from Winston Weisman in 1975–1986.

Figure 105. *Arcading at top of 'tower,'* 484-90 Broome Street, New York City. Photograph by Vaughn L. Glasgow and M. Greenberg, 1971. (Neg. no. Weisman roll 35)

The "Pennsylvania State University-National Science Foundation Project SoHo" documented the architectural history of hundreds of structures, many of which became part of the SoHo (South of Houston) Historic District in 1973. Although cast-iron structures predominate, the building at 484 Broome Street, erected in 1890 by architect Alfred Zucker, includes brick and brownstone towers.

Figure 106. Fifth Avenue between 116th and 117th streets, New York City. Glass negative by Edward Wenzel, 1893. (Neg. no. 1092)

This photograph shows an area of Harlem a few blocks north of Central Park during its transition from shanties (foreground) to apartment buildings and rowhouses (background). The Society's files include the title "Home of the High Rock Gang" for this glass negative.

74. EDWARD WENZEL PHOTOGRAPH COLLECTION
1892–1925, bulk ca. 1895–ca. 1905.
ca. 250 glass negatives (4 × 5 in., 5 × 7 in., and 8 × 10 in.) and several photographic prints.

Part-time photographer Edward Wenzel shared an interest in history with active Society member and archaeologist William L. Calver. Most of Wenzel's well-captioned photographs portray buildings and sites associated with the Revolutionary War era in the New York City, Hudson River, New Jersey, and Philadelphia regions. Wenzel's 8 × 10 in. glass negatives from the 1890s depict areas of upper Manhattan, including the Inwood Valley, Washington Heights, Spuyten Duyvil Creek, the Harlem River, and the home of the High Rock Gang on Fifth Avenue (Figure 106). There are also scenes of the last oxen team at work in New York City (on a Staten Island farm), of a mountaineer family at Ramapo Mountain, and of the dirigible hangar at Lakehurst, New Jersey.

Arrangement and access: The negatives are filed by assigned numbers. A finding aid lists each negative by place, title, and date. Entries in the Photographer Reference Index identify the negative number ranges and summarize subject coverage. Several vintage and numerous modern prints can be found in the Geographic File.
Provenance: Gift from William L. Calver in 1924, with additions from Edward Wenzel in 1925.

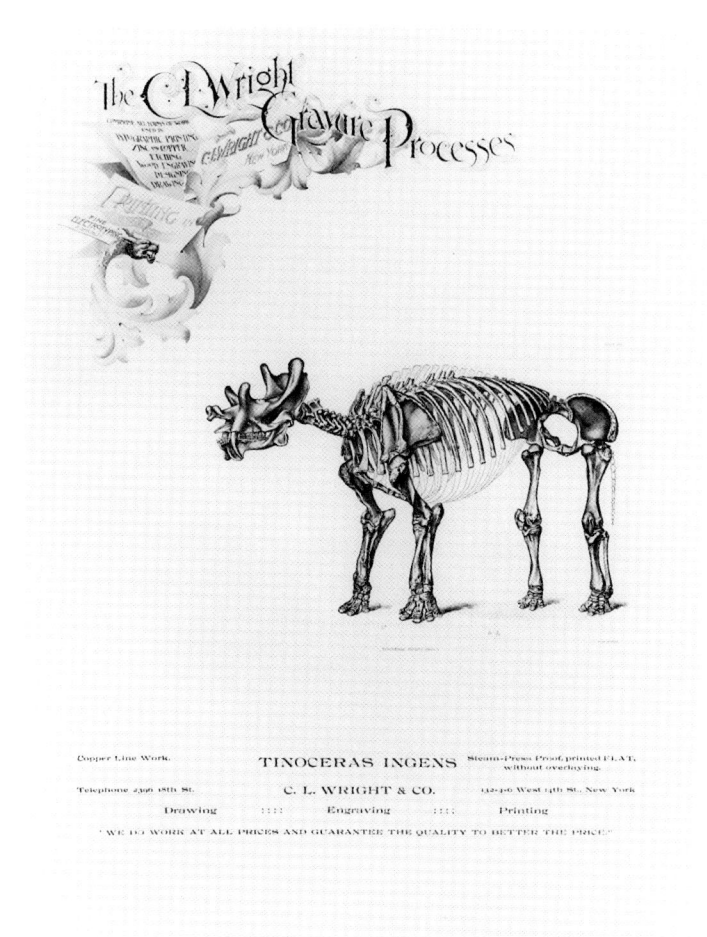

Figure 107. Letterhead for C.L. Wright & Co., New York City, ca. 1900. (Neg. no. 71152)

The company stationery advertised the firm's varied services with examples of its sharply detailed printing work. Although this stationery might have been designed after C.L. Wright's son began to run the firm, the precise lines and shading in the skeleton of the Tinoceras Ingens reflect the founder's values: appreciation of fine drawing and tireless efforts to develop better photomechanical printing processes. C.L. Wright told his son "nothing but the best was good enough and 'good enough' was no good at all." ("Charles Lennox Wright" by Stephen H. Horgan in *Photo-Engravers Bulletin,* March 1927, p. 49)

75. CHARLES LENNOX WRIGHT PHOTOMECHANICAL PRINTING COLLECTION
ca. 1850–1950, bulk 1880–1905.
ca. 500 black-and-white and color photomechanical prints, ca. 20 photographs, ca. 20 drawings, and 10 pieces of printing equipment. Accompanied by 82-page handwritten biography and catalog.

Charles Lennox Wright (1852–1901) was descended from two similarly named engravers: his father, Charles Washington Wright, and his grandfather, Charles Cushing Wright. A native New Yorker, he began his career in commercial picture reproduction in 1869 at *Frank Leslie's Illustrated Newspaper.* Experimentation to create economical, high-fidelity reproductions from artists' drawings and from photographs was widespread during the mid-1800s, and subsequent jobs exposed

Wright to many methods for producing printing plates. According to his son and biographer, each experience contributed to his development of a commercially viable, typographically compatible, zinc etching technique that helped revolutionize book and magazine illustration in the early 1880s. Relief zinc etching, also called line photoengraving, reproduces line drawings faithfully through photomechanical means (rather than hand engraving). In 1885, Ben Day helped Wright start the C.L. Wright Zincogravure Company. Joseph Pennell was among the artists who admired the superior quality of Wright's work, much of which was published in *Century Magazine*. Wright also introduced improvements in copper etched halftone and four-color halftone work before his death at age 49 (Figure 107). His son, Charles Lennox Wright, II (born 1876), took an active role in the company beginning in 1897, but he preferred to work as a painter, and the company closed by 1905.

Wright, II, assembled this collection ca. 1950 to demonstrate his father's achievements, which have been little recognized. He compiled an unpublished biography that also chronicles the transition from wood engraved to photomechanical illustrations and explains the steps in zinc line etching and copper halftone etching. Proof prints and pages from magazines document many stages of his father's career: collotypes made for Edward Bierstadt, wash-out gelatines for John C. Moss, art facsimile photolithographs for J.H. Bufford's Sons, and several types of color halftones. Of special interest are the notes written on many prints to identify what are usually anonymous printing companies and processes. Heavily represented illustrators include Edwin A. Abbey, Jules Guérin, Maxfield Parrish, and Howard Pyle. The collection also contains technical drawings of printing equipment sketched by Wright's son from memory; a 400-line halftone printing screen; portraits of associates; and family photographs.

Arrangement and access: The material is filed by size and type (e.g., small prints; family photographs; large prints; printing equipment). The finding aid summarizes the material in each filing category. The catalog in the biography (pp. 38-82) describes each item in detail and explains its significance.
Provenance: Gift from Charles L. Wright, II, in 1952.
References: Charles L. Wright, II, "The Pioneer of Zinc Etching: Introduction to the Charles Lennox Wright I Collection," *The New-York Historical Society Quarterly* 36 (April 1952): 194-209.
Related: The Manuscript Department, Reading Room, and Department of Paintings, Sculpture, and Decorative Arts also have Wright family material.

The Indexes

Figures 108 and 109. Aftermath of the Blizzard of 1888, New York City. Photographs by unidentified photographer. At right, a pedestrian leans against a wall of snow at Madison Avenue south from 50th Street. (Geographic File, neg. no. 3387) Below, two men trudge through deep snow beneath downed electrical wires on Wall Street. (Geographic File, neg. no. 9828)

Chronological Index

Researchers interested in a particular time period can use this chronological index table to identify which collections depict people, places, or events during that era. The dates refer to the time period depicted in the images (not the years in which the material was created). Collection and file names are abbreviated.

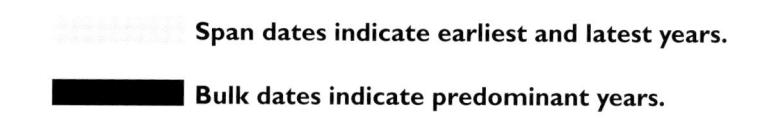

Span dates indicate earliest and latest years.

Bulk dates indicate predominant years.

COLLECTION NAME	YEARS 1500 1700 1750 1800 1825 1850 1875 1900 1925 1950 1975 2000
Albok	
Album	
Architect	
Beals	
Billboard	
Bookplate	
Boyd	
Bracklow	
Browning	
Caricature	
Carte de visite	
Cased photos	

Figure 110. King of Diamonds card in deck of playing cards that advertises Murphy Varnish. Lithograph by A. Dougherty & Co., 1883. (Graphic Arts File, neg. no 61309)

Figure 111. *May Parties in Cent[ral] Park, N.Y.* Photograph attributed to John S. Johnston, ca 1895. (Geographic File, neg. no. 51800)

Span dates indicate earliest and latest years.

Bulk dates indicate predominant years.

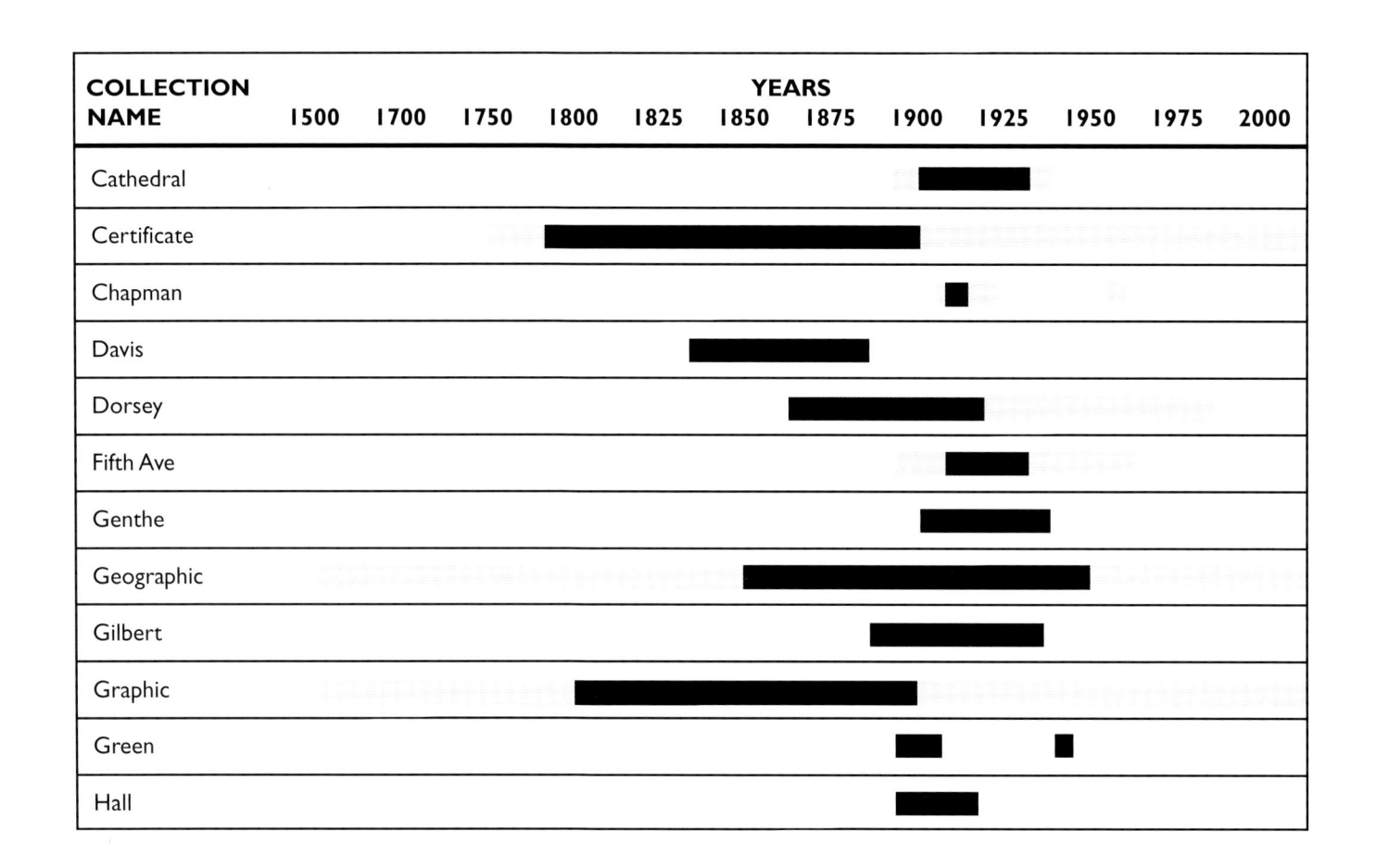

COLLECTION NAME	1500	1700	1750	1800	1825	1850	YEARS 1875	1900	1925	1950	1975	2000
Cathedral												
Certificate												
Chapman												
Davis												
Dorsey												
Fifth Ave												
Genthe												
Geographic												
Gilbert												
Graphic												
Green												
Hall												

Figure 112. *The Last Bather: Close of the Bathing Season at Manhattan Beach.* Color lithograph drawn by Joseph Keppler and published in *Puck*, September 15, 1880. (Keppler Collection, neg. no. 70803)

Figure 113. *Try Rice's Seeds.* Lithograph by Cosack & Co., Buffalo and Chicago, ca. 1870. (Landauer Collection, neg. no. 34789)

COLLECTION NAME	YEARS 1500 – 2000
Havemeyer	ca. 1840–1900
Hewitt	ca. 1925
Hyde	ca. 1700–1800
Ingalls	ca. 1875–1925
Keppler	ca. 1850–1900
Kilmer	ca. 1925–1950
Landauer	ca. 1840–1925
Lawrence	ca. 1850
LeBoeuf	ca. 1820–1875
Levick	ca. 1925
Liberman (Wall St.)	ca. 1825–1925
Liberman (Worship)	ca. 1950

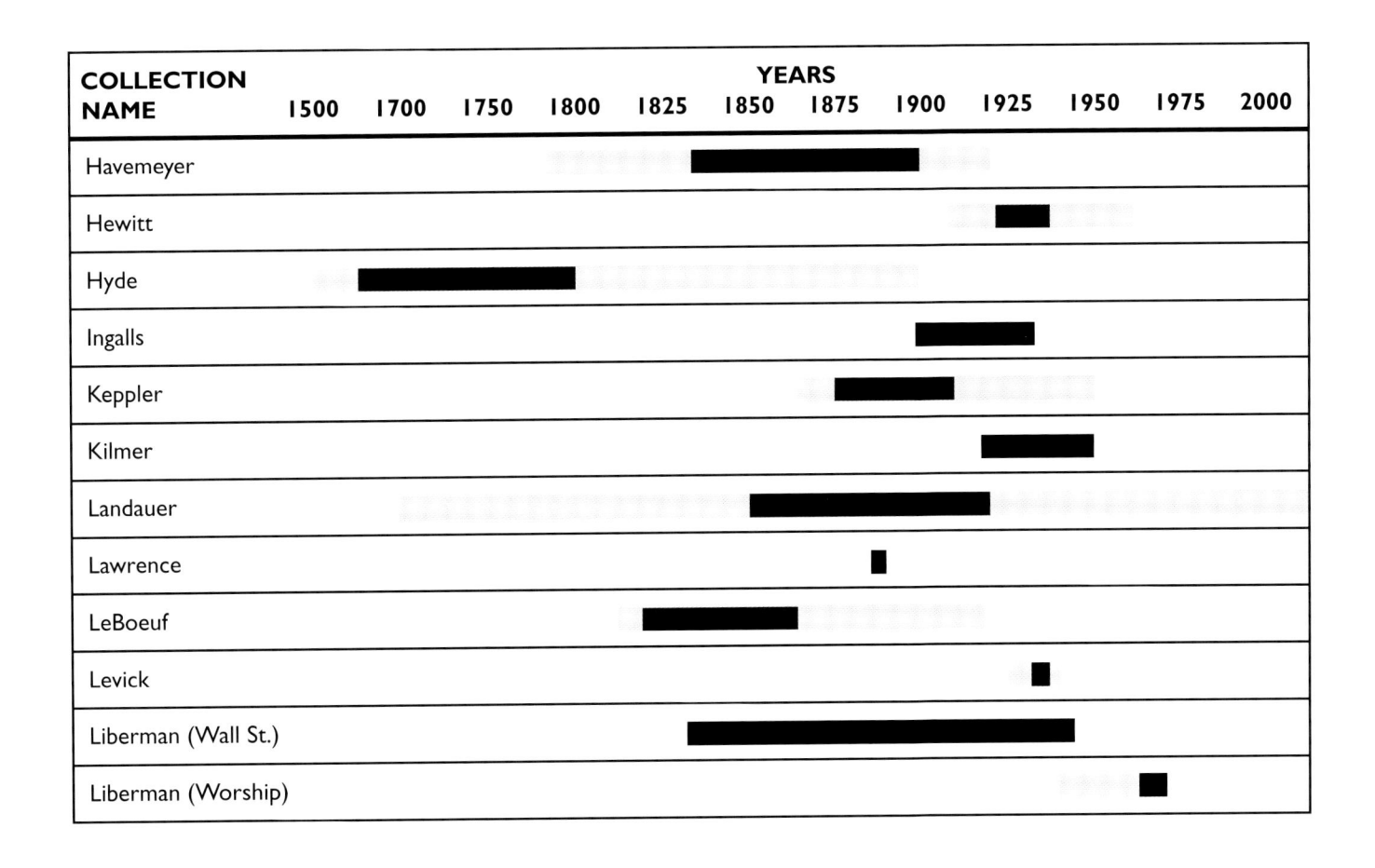

161

Figure 114. New York City Hall, Manhattan. Front elevation. Wash drawing by Joseph Mangin and John McComb, Jr., 1802. (McComb Collection, neg. no. 18986)

Figure 115. Sculptor John Rogers (1829-1904) in his New York City studio. Photograph by unidentified photographer, ca. 1864. (Portrait File, neg. no. 26484)

Span dates indicate earliest and latest years.

Bulk dates indicate predominant years.

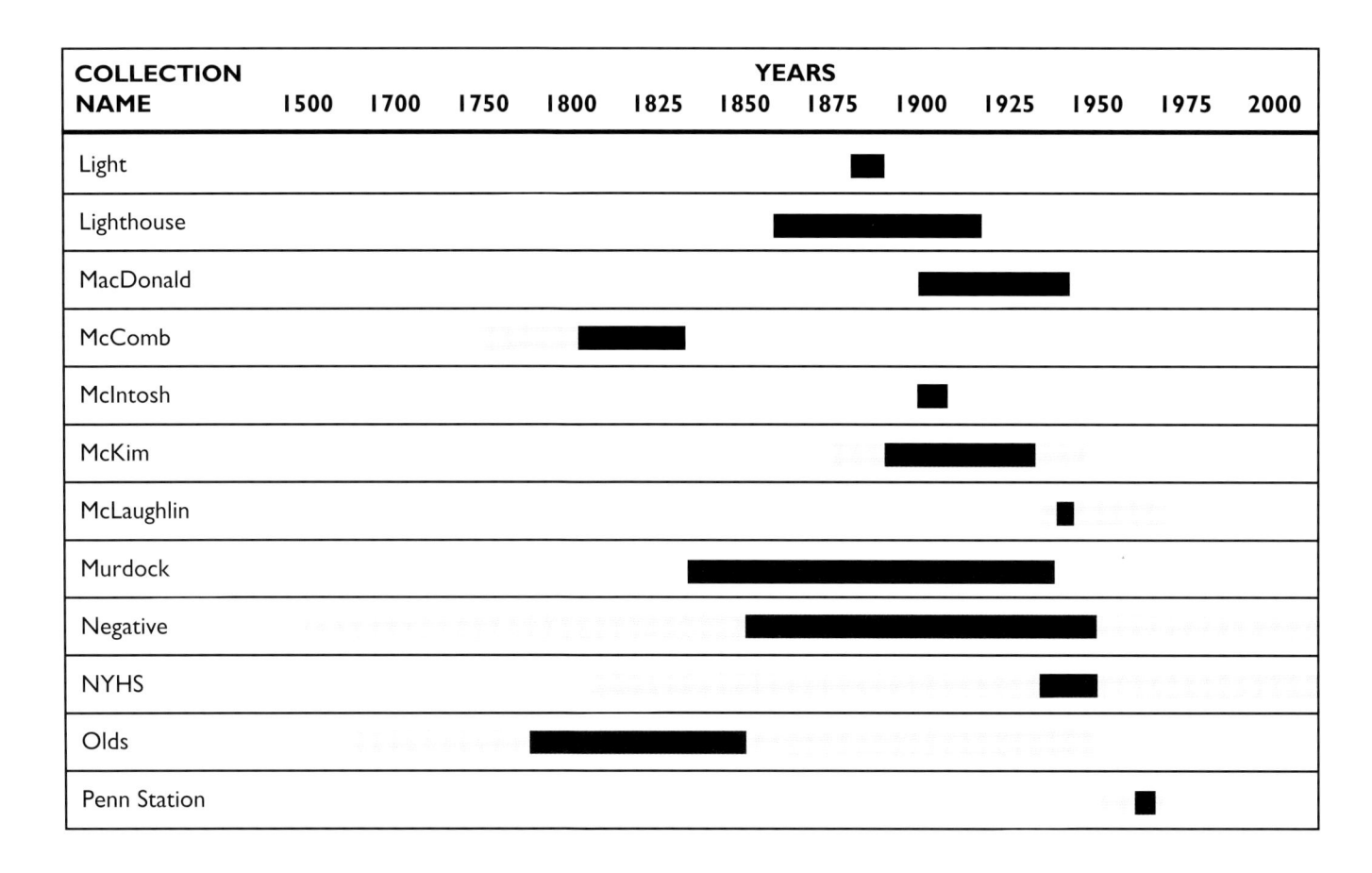

COLLECTION NAME	1500	1700	1750	1800	1825	1850	1875	1900	1925	1950	1975	2000
Light							■					
Lighthouse						▬▬▬▬▬▬▬▬▬▬						
MacDonald								▬▬▬▬▬▬				
McComb				▬▬▬▬								
McIntosh							■					
McKim							▬▬▬▬▬					
McLaughlin										■		
Murdock					▬▬▬▬▬▬▬▬▬▬▬							
Negative						▬▬▬▬▬▬▬▬▬▬▬▬▬						
NYHS										▬		
Olds				▬▬▬▬▬▬▬▬								
Penn Station										■		

162

Figure 116. Street Arabs in sleeping quarters at night, Mulberry Street, New York City. Photograph attributed to Jacob Riis, late 1880s. (Riis Collection, neg. no. 70225)

Figure 117. Spring in West Burnside Avenue near Osborne Place looking west, Bronx, New York. Photograph by James Reuel Smith, October 7, 1897. (Smith Collection, neg. no. 63813-K70)

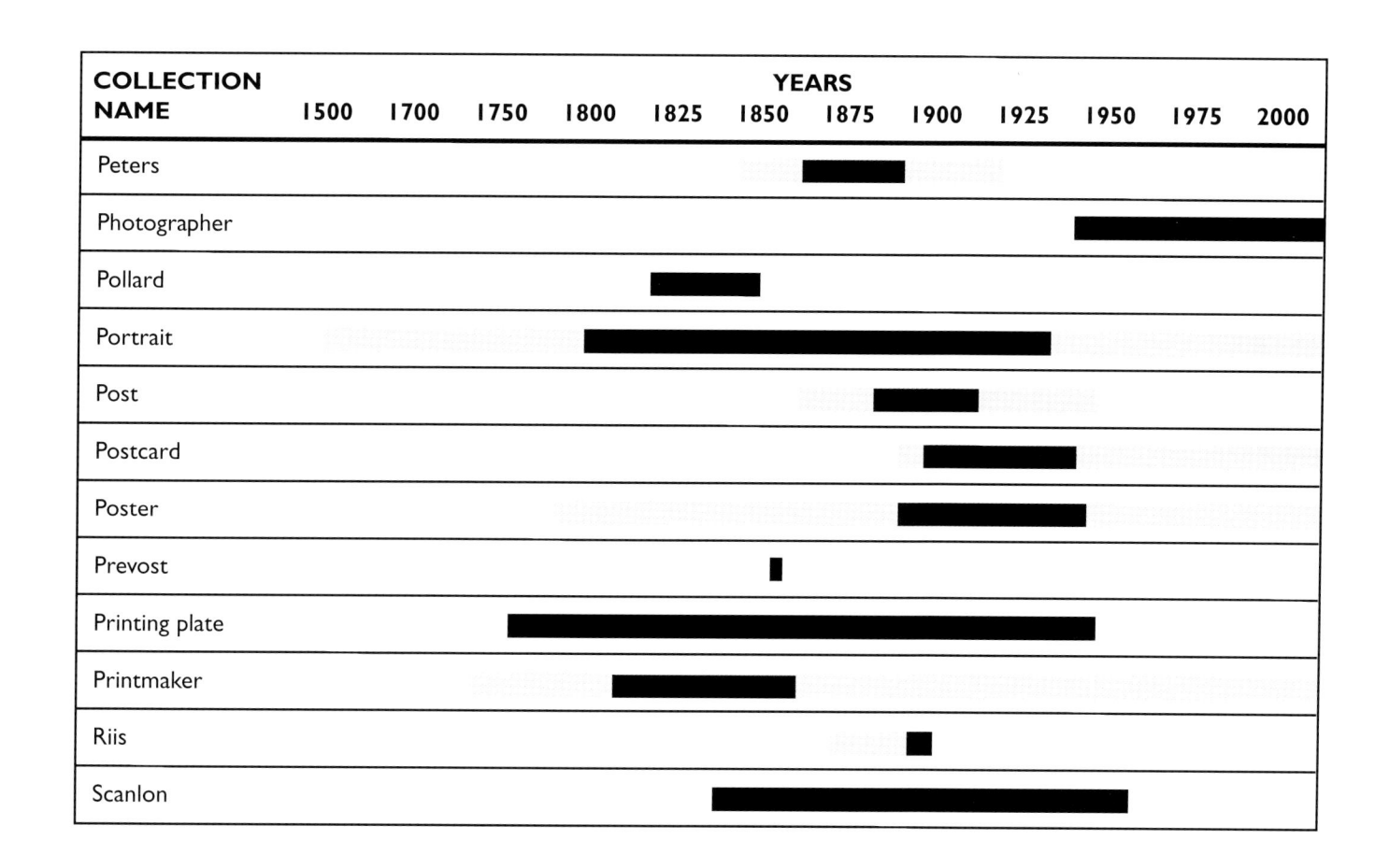

COLLECTION NAME	1500	1700	1750	1800	1825	1850	1875	1900	1925	1950	1975	2000
Peters							███					
Photographer											████	████
Pollard					███							
Portrait				█████████████████								
Post							████					
Postcard								████				
Poster								████	████			
Prevost					█							
Printing plate			████████████████████████									
Printmaker				██████								
Riis							█					
Scanlon						████████████████						

163

Figure 118. View from Lexington Avenue between 45th and 46th Streets, New York City. Looking west with Grand Central Terminal in rear. Stereograph by unidentified photographer, ca. 1873. (Stereograph File, neg. no. 20573)

Span dates indicate earliest and latest years.

Bulk dates indicate predominant years.

COLLECTION NAME	YEARS 1500 1700 1750 1800 1825 1850 1875 1900 1925 1950 1975 2000
Silver	
Smith	
Smyth	
Snook	
Stereograph	
Stonebridge	
Strobridge	
Subject	
Subway	
Transparency	
Trappan	
Ulmann	
Weisman	
Wenzel	
Wright	

Figure 119. Lower Hudson Street, New York City.
Photograph by Marcus Ormsbee, ca. 1865.
(Geographic File, neg. no. 16930)

Figure 120. Pickle peddler and customer, New York City. Photograph by Browning, 1930s. (Browning Collection, neg. no. 58430)

General Index

The general index lists key subjects, creators, media, and donors, as well as collection names and the *Guide*'s illustrations. Some collections and files cover more topics than can be individually indexed here. For example, the index entry for Pennsylvania Station points to the Levick and Pennsylvania Station Demolition Photograph Collections, but not to the Geographic File or the McKim, Mead & White Collection, which include Penn Station images among hundreds of other topics.

NOTE: Index numbers refer to the entry numbers for the Collections, except for numbers in parentheses, which refer to pages in the introduction and indexes. Collection entry names are bold-faced.

A

Abbey (Edwin A.), 75
Adirondack Mountains, 2, 54
Advertisements, 5, 17, 20, 31, 55, 65, 68 *(161)*
Aerial photographs, 43
Africa, 27
African Americans, 11, 12, 30, 49, 68, 72
Albertype Co., 54
Albok (John), 1
Albok Photograph Collection, 1 *(25)*
Album File, 2 *(2, 23)*
Albumen photographs. *See* Photographs
Albums, 2, 8, 29, 36, 42, 44, 51, 53, 61, 69
Alden (Albert), 68
Alland (Alexander), 8, 50, 59
Allegories, 6, 27, 68
Amateur photographers, 8, 28, 32, 36, 37, 62, 63, 65, 70, 71
Ambrotypes. *See* Photographs
America, 27
American Art Union, 58
Anderson (Alexander), 57, 58 *(16)*
Anson (Rufus), 12
Anthony (E. & H.T.), 2, 11, 65
Appalachia, 72
Appleton (D. & Co.), 11
Aquatints. *See* Prints
Architect and Engineer File, 3 *(26)*
Architects. *See* Bulfinch (Charles); Carrère & Hastings; Davis (Alexander J.); Delano & Aldrich; Flagg (Ernest); Gambrill (Charles D.); Gilbert (Cass); Haviland (John); Hood (Raymond M.); Jennings (Arthur B.); Kendall (William M.); Lawrence (Jacob); Mangin (Joseph F.); Martens (James); McComb (John, Jr.); McComb (John, Sr.); McKim, Mead, & White; Peabody & Stearns; Pollard (Calvin); Post (George B.); Post (William S.); Renwick (James, Jr.); Richardson (William S.); Rosborg (Christian F.); Schermerhorn & Foulks; Snook (John B); Strickland (William); Trench (Joseph); Trumbull (John); Upjohn (Richard); Vaux (Calvert); Warren & Wetmore; York and Sawyer
Architectural drawings, 3, 16, 21, 40, 42, 46, 51, 53, 64 *(26)*
Architectural photographs, 3, 13, 20, 21, 23, 26, 38, 42, 43, 48, 53, 61, 69, 73 *(25)*
Architectural records, 21, 42, 53, 64
Armbruster (Eugene L.), 20 *(31)*
Artists. *See* Abbey (Edwin A.); Audubon (John J.); Bartlett (William H.); Beckwith (James Carroll); Cary (W.M.); Darley (F.O.C.); Durand (Asher B.); Durr (Louis); Edouart (Auguste); Ferriss (Hugh); French (Daniel Chester); Frost (A.B.); Gould (Joseph J.); Guérin (Jules); Homer (Winslow); Johnson (Thomas R.); Keppler (Joseph and Joseph, Jr.); Lefferts (Charles M.); Milbert (Jacques); Miller (William Rickarby); Mount (William Sidney); Nast (Thomas); Ogden (Harry A.); Opper (Frederick B.); Parrish (Maxfield); Penfield (Edward); Remington (Frederic); Saint-Mémin (Charles Balthazar Julien Févret de); Sargeant (Edward A.); Shaw (Joshua); Wall (William G.); Worth (Thomas); Yewell (George Henry); Young (Art)
Asia, 27
A.T. Stewart Store, 64
Audubon (John J.), 58 *(30)*

B

Bachmann (John), 20
Bagoe (George T.), 65, 68 *(31)*
Baillie (James), 10
Baker & Godwin, 55
Banks. *See* Buildings, commercial
Barnard & Gibson, 11
Barnum & Bailey, 67 *(36)*
Bartlett (William H.), 22
Baseball, 32, 34 *(4)*
Beaches, 66 *(13, 161)*
Beals (Jessie Tarbox), 4
Beals Photograph Collection, 4 *(12, 25)*
Beck & Pauli, 20
Beckwith (James Carroll), 22
Beekman family, 12
Bennett (William J.), 57, 58 *(30)*
Beseler (Charles Co.), 70

167

Bien (Julius), 38
Bierstadt (Edward), 75
Bierstadts, 65
Billboard Photograph Collection, 5 (25)
Billboards, 5
Blizzards, 20, 32, 37 (158)
Blueprints. See Architectural drawings
Blumenthal (Hermann), 64 (31)

Figure 121. Bookplate for Bella C. Landauer. Engraving designed by William P. Barrett, 1926. (Bookplate File, neg. no. 61280)

Board of Transportation of New York City, 69
Boats. See Transportation, ships
Bogardus (Abraham), 12
Bolton (Reginald P.), 2
Bookmarks. See Ephemera
Bookplate File, 6 (16, 28, 168)
Bookplates. See Ephemera
Borne (Mortimer), 7
Bowen (Mrs. G.M.), 68
Boyd (Agnes Gray), 7

Boyd Collection of New York City Prints, 7 (28)
Boyd (James), 7 (18)
Brabyn (Claude and Mrs.), 29
Bracklow Photograph Collection, 8 (12, 13, 19, 21, 25)
Bracklow (Robert L.), 8 (21)
Brady (Mathew B.), 2, 11, 12, 68 (31)
Briem (Gottlob L.), 7, 57
Britton & Rey, 22
Broadsides. See Ephemera
Broadway (NYC), 69
Bronx (NYC). See New York City
Brooklyn (NYC). See New York City
Brooklyn Bridge, 31
Brown (James W.), 6
Browne (Syd), 7
Browning (Irving), 9
Browning Photograph Collection, 9 (6, 25, 166)
Browning (Sam), 9
Bryan (Thomas J.), 22
Bufford (John H.), 20, 75
Buildings, 2-5, 7-9, 15, 16, 20, 21, 23, 24, 26, 28, 32, 34-38, 40, 42, 43, 45, 46, 49-51, 53, 54, 56, 59, 61-66, 69, 70, 73, 74
    commercial, 2, 9, 21, 24, 35, 36, 40, 43, 51, 53, 56, 61, 64, 69, 73 (165, 175)
    educational, 53
    hotels, 9, 17, 53, 54
    interiors, 2, 9, 13, 20, 26, 61 (32)
    military, 40
    monuments, 14, 16, 51
    public, 16, 21, 36, 40, 42, 46, 51, 53
    religious, 13, 16, 21, 36, 40, 51
    residential, 2, 3, 9, 16, 21, 26, 36, 42, 43, 51, 53, 64, 69
    skyscrapers, 9, 28, 53, 73
Bulfinch (Charles), 3
Burger (Chester), 70
Burgis (William), 58
Burr McIntosh Monthly, 41
Burton (Thomas J.), 70 (31)
Buses. See Transportation
Businesses. See Buildings, commercial
Butler (George H.), 31

NOTE: Index numbers refer to the entry numbers for the Collections, except for numbers in parentheses, which refer to pages in the introduction and indexes. Collection entry names are bold-faced.

C

Cabinet cards. See Photographs
Cabinet officers, 25
Caesar, 12
Calendars. See Ephemera
California, 10
Calling cards. See Ephemera
Calotypes. See Photographs
Calver (William), 46, 74
Camera clubs, 8, 13, 28, 30, 32
Canada, 54
Canoune (Howard M.), 2 (2)
Carbutt (John), 65
Caricature and Cartoon File, 10 (28)
Caricatures and cartoons, 2, 10, 11, 27, 29, 31, 47, 49, 57 (161). See also Humorous images
Carrère & Hastings, 3
Carstensen and Gildemeister, 46
Carte de Visite File, 11 (23)
Cartes de visite. See Photographs
Cartoons. See Caricatures and cartoons
Cary (W.M.), 49
Cased Photograph File, 12 (23)
Cast-iron buildings, 64, 73
Cathedral Church of St. John the Divine Photograph Collection, 13 (25)
Cats, 19, 62
Celebrations. See Parades and celebrations
Central Park (NYC) 1 (34, 160)
Century Magazine, 75
Certificate File, 14 (28)
Certificates. See Ephemera
Chapman (Arthur D.), 15
Chapman Photograph Collection, 15 (25)
Child (Edmund B.), 20, 52 (31)
Children, 41, 49, 52, 62 (163)
Chinatown (NYC), 19, 32
Chinatown (San Francisco, CA), 19
Chromolithographs. See Prints
Churches. See Buildings, religious
Cigar box labels. See Ephemera
Cigarette packages. See Ephemera
Circus, 11, 55, 67, 68 (36)
City life. See Street scenes
Civil War, 2, 11, 22, 49, 55, 65, 68
Clay (Edward W.), 10
Clipper ship cards. See Ephemera
Clippings, 2, 17, 18, 21, 29, 42, 44, 47, 53
Clothing, 31, 68. See also Fashion photographs, Fashion prints, Portraits
Coleman (Daniel), 70

Colleges. *See* Buildings, educational
Collingwood (Helen A.), 40
Color photographs. *See* Photographs
Colorado, 17
Comic strips, 10
Coney Island (NYC), 8, 24 (13)
Connecticut, 21
Construction work, 2, 9, 69
Cooper (Peter) family, 12
Correspondence, 6, 21, 31, 42, 53
Cotterell (Harry, Jr.), 45
Cozzens (Isaccher), 22
Croton Reservoir, 8
Crystal Palace (23)
Cuba, 2, 41
Cunningham (Bill), 50
Currier (Nathaniel), 25, 68
Currier & Ives, 10, 20, 47, 58, 6
Cyanotpyes. *See* Photographs

D

Daguerreotypes. *See* Photographs
Dance, 19, 31
Darley (F.O.C.), 57
Davenport (Homer C.), 10
D'Avignon (Francis), 25
Davis (Alexander J.), 16, 58
Davis Architectural Drawing Collection, 16 (26)
Dawkins (Henry), 6, 14, 57
De Groot family, 12
DeForest (Henry P.), 6
Dehmann (Karl), 7, 35
Delano & Aldrich, 3
Delano family, 12
Design drawings, 6, 40, 67, 75
Detroit Publishing Co., 44, 54
DeVoe (Thomas F.), 2
Dewey Arch, 8
Disasters, 49, 63, 65, 66
Dodd (George C.), 70 (31)
Donaldson Brothers, 31
Dorsey Collection of Pictorial Clippings, 17 (28)
Dorsey (Leslie), 17
Drawings, 10, 40 *See also* Architectural drawings, Design drawings, Engineering drawings, Landscape architecture drawings
Drucker & Baltes Co., 5
Dry goods, 31
Drypoints. *See* Prints

Dunsmore (John Ward) (31)
Durand (Asher B.), 58
Durr (Louis), 22
Dutcher (H.F.), 23

E

Edouart (Auguste), 52
Education, 14. *See also* Buildings, educational
Elevated railroads. *See* Transportation
Endicott & Co., 20 (170)
Engineering drawings, 3, 40, 51
Engravings. *See* Prints
Ephemera, 2, 6, 14, 17, 18, 22, 25, 29, 31, 46, 55, 68 (28)
    bookmarks, 31
    bookplates, 6
    broadsides, 31
    calendars, 22
    calling cards, 57
    certificates, 14, 22, 46
    cigar box labels, 31
    cigarette packages, 31
    clipper ship cards, 22
    fans, 31
    fraktur illuminations, 22
    games, 22
    greeting cards, 54
    handbills, 31, 68
    labels, 6, 31
    lottery tickets, 31
    matchbook covers, 31
    paper roses, 22
    paper weights, 31
    patriotic envelopes, 22
    pictorial lettersheets, 22
    playbills, 55
    playing cards, 22 (160)
    rewards of merit, 14
    sheet music covers, 25, 31
    speakeasy cards, 31 (29)
    tobacco tins, 31
    trade cards, 31
    trade catalogs, 31
    watchpapers, 31
Equitable Life Assurance Society Bldg., 53, 63
Etchings. *See* Prints
Ethnic groups, 1
Europe, 27, 55, 68
Expositions, 17, 54, 65

F

Fairs. *See* Expositions
Families, 2, 66 (2)
Fans. *See* Ephemera
Fashion photographs, 4
Fashion prints, 17, 49, 68
Feininger (Andreas), 50 (23)
Ferries. *See* Transportation
Ferriss (Hugh), 21
Field Exploration Committee, 46 (17)
Fifth Avenue (NYC), 74

Figure 122. Experiment with a folding top for a double-decker bus, New York City. Photograph by American Studio, 1919. (Fifth Avenue Coach Company Collection, neg. no. 58506)

Fifth Avenue Coach Company Photograph Collection, 18 (25, 169)
Fires and firefighters, 14, 20, 63
Flagg (Ernest), 3
Food and beverages, 31
Forbes (Esther), 72
Fort George, 58
Fortifications. *See* Buildings, Military
Four Continents, 27
Four Indian Kings, 68 (27)
Fraktur illuminations. *See* Ephemera
Frank Leslie's Illustrated Newspaper, 49
Franklin (Benjamin), 27
Fredericks (Charles D.), 11, 12

French (Daniel Chester), 8, 21
French (Edwin D.), 6
Fridenberg (Robert), 52
Frost (A.B.), 49
Fulton (Robert), 33

G

Gallatin (Albert), 52
Gambee (Robert), 50
Gambrill (Charles D.), 53
Games. See Ephemera
Gardens, 4, 26
Gardner (Alexander), 2
Genthe (Arnold), 19
Genthe Photograph Collection, 19 *(19, 23-25)*
Geographic File, 20 *(10, 14, 22, 158, 160, 165, 175)* See also New York City, Street scenes, Views
George Washington Bridge (NYC), 20 *(14)*
Gerdau (Carl), 70
Gilbert Architectural Record Collection, 21 *(15, 19, 26)*
Gilbert (Cass), 21
Gilbert (Cass, Jr.), 21
Gilbert Elevated Railway, 3
Gilbert (Emily), 21
Godwin (Abraham), 14
Goelet (Robert G.), 52 *(19)*
Gold rush, 10, 22
Golinkin (Joseph), 35
Gould (Joseph J.), 55
Grand Central Depot (NYC), 64
Graphic arts, 6, 22
Graphic Arts File, 22 *(28, 160)*
Great Depression, 9
Green Collection of Elevated Railroad Photographs, 23 *(25)*
Green (Norvin H.), 23
Greenwich Village (NYC), 4, 15
Greeting cards. See Ephemera
Guérin (Jules), 21, 75
Gurney (Jeremiah), 11, 12

Figure 123. *The Steamer Mary Powell.* (Shown on the Hudson River, New York.) Colored lithograph by Endicott & Co., N.Y., ca. 1880. (Subject File, neg. no 43113)

H

Hall (George P.), 24
Hall (James S.), 24
Hall Photograph Collection, 24 *(19, 25)*
Hancock (John), 52
Handbills. See Ephemera
Harbors, 20, 33, 43, 44, 60
Harlem (NYC), 5, 36
Harlow (Alvin F.), 20
Harper's Weekly, 49, 55
Harrison (William Henry), 25
Hassam (Childe), 35
Hassler (William D.), *(31, 32)*
Hatos (Alexander), 48 *(25)*
Havell (Robert, Jr.), 58
Havemeyer Collection of Portrait Prints, 25 *(18, 28)*
Havemeyer (Henry O.), 25
Haviland (John), 3
Haynes (F. Jay), 65
Heraldry, 6, 14
Hervey (Anoinette B.), 13 *(12, 19, 25)*
Hester Street (NYC), *(10)*
Hewitt (Abram S.) family, 12
Hewitt and Smith Photograph Collection, 26 *(12, 25)*
Hewitt (Mattie E.), 26
Hill (John), 58
Hiller (Joseph, Sr.), 52

Himely (Sigismond), 57
Hine (Charles G.), *(31)*
Hoff (Henry), 58
Hoffman (Samuel V.), 16, 51, 56 *(18)*
Holmes (Silas), 12
Homer (Winslow), 49
Hood (Raymond M.), 3
Hotels. See Buildings, hotels
Houses. See Buildings, residential
Houses of Worship Collection, 36
Huberland (Morris), 50
Hudson River area (NY), 16, 20, 43, 44, 68
Hudson River Day Line, 68
Humorous images, 6, 54, 65 See also Caricatures and cartoons
Hunter (F. Leo), 7
Huntington (Collis P.), 53
Hyde Collection of Allegorical Prints of the Four Continents, 27 *(28)*
Hyde (James H.), 27

I

Illustrated newspapers, 49
Illustrations, 17, 22, 25, 49, 57, 68, 75
Imbert (Anthony), 57
Immigrants, 49, 59
Indians. See Native Americans
Ingalls (Frank M.), 28
Ingalls Photograph Collection, 28 *(25)*
Interior decorators, 26
Interiors. See Buildings

NOTE: Index numbers refer to the entry numbers for the Collections, except for numbers in parentheses, which refer to pages in the introduction and indexes. Collection entry names are bold-faced.

J

Jackson (Andrew), 10, 25
Jackson (William H.), 65
Jamestown (NY), 20
Jennings (Arthur B.), 3
Johnson (Thomas R.), 21
Johnson (William) testimonial, 14
Johnston (David Claypoole), 10
Johnston (John S.), 20, 24, 45 (160)

K

Karoly (Andrew), 35
Keep (Austin Baxter) (31)
Kelloggs, 68
Kendall (William M.), 42
Keppler Cartoon Collection, 29 (28, 161)
Keppler (Joseph), 29
Keppler (Joseph, Jr.), 29
Keppler (Joseph, Jr., Mrs.), 29
Keystone View Co., 65
Kilburn Brothers, 65
Kilmer Portrait Photograph Collection, 30 (12, 25)
Kilmer (Theron W.), 30
King Features Syndicate, 10
Kodak prints. See Photographs, Kodak
Kurz & Allison, 68

L

Labels. See Ephemera
Landscape architecture drawings, 3
Landscape photographs, 72
Landauer (Bella C.), 6, 31 (18, 168)
Landauer Collection of Bookplates, 6
Landauer Collection of Business and Advertising Ephemera, 31 (28, 29, 161)
Langenheim Brothers, 65
Langill Photo Co., 24
Lankes (Julius J.), 6
Lantern slides. See Photographs, transparencies
Lawrence (Jacob), 40
Lawrence (James), 68
Lawrence Photograph Collection, 32 (4, 12, 25)
Lawrence (Richard H.), 8, 32, 59
LeBoeuf Collection of Robert Fulton Prints, 33 (28, 30)
LeBoeuf (Randall J., Jr.), 33
Lefferts (Charles M.), 68
Leidersdorf & Co., 31
Lens (Bernard), (27)
Leslie's Illustrated Newspaper, 49
Lester (Robert M.), 70
Levick (Edwin), 34
Levick Studio, 34
Levick Studio Photograph Collection, 34 (25)
Lexington Avenue (NYC), 69 (164)
Liberman Collection of Wall Street Prints, 35 (28)
Liberman (Herman N.), 35, 36
Liberman Photograph Collection, 36 (25)
Libraries, 6
Light Collection of New York City Photographs, 37 (25)
Light (William E.), 37
Lighthouse Photograph and Print Collection, 38 (25)
Lighthouses, 38, 40
Lincoln (Abraham), 2, 25, 31
Lind (Jenny), 52
Linoleum prints. See Prints
Litchfield (Edward S.), 16
Lithographs. See Prints
Logan (Robert E.), 63
Logbooks. See Photographs, Logbooks
Long Island (NY), 3, 8, 19, 20, 24, 44, 71
Longacre (James B.), 25
Loonan (Alfred C.), 65
Lottery tickets. See Ephemera
Lowell (Nat), 35
Lower East Side (NYC), 9, 32, 59 (11)

M

Macdonald (Arthur N.), 6
MacDonald (Pirie), 39
MacDonald (Pirie, Mrs.), 39
MacDonald Portrait Photograph Collection, 39 (12, 19, 25, 172)
Mackey (Chris), 50
Magazine posters, 55
Magee (J.L.), 10
Magnus (Charles), 22
Magri (Countess), 2
Maine, 38
Mangin (Joseph F.), 40
Manhattan (NYC). See New York City
Maps, 57
Maritime relief associations, 14
Martens (James W.), 3 (19)
Matchbook covers. See Ephemera
Maverick family, 6, 58
McComb Architecural Drawing Collection, 40 (17, 26, 162)
McComb (John, Jr.), 40
McComb (John, Sr.), 40
McCullough (Hall Park), 22 (19)
McIntosh (Burr), 41
McIntosh Photograph Collection, 41 (12, 19, 25)
McKim (Charles Follen), 42
McKim, Mead & White Architectural Record Collection, 42 (19, 26, 171)
McLaughlin Air Service, 43
McLaughlin Air Service Photograph Collection, 43 (25)
McNulty (William C.), 7
Mead (William Rutherford), 42
Men, 30, 39, 52
Meserve (Frederick Hill), 2
Metropolitan Museum of Art, 38
Metropolitan Opera (NYC), 17
Metropolitan Transportation Authority, 18
Mezzotints. See Prints
Mexican War, 68
Mielatz (Charles F.W.), 7
Milbert (Jacques), 58
Military buildings. See Buildings

Figure 124. *Proposed fountain at entrance to Prospect Park, intersection of Fifteenth Street and Ninth Avenue, Brooklyn.* Watercolor, ca 1908. (Mckim, Mead & White Collection, neg. no 60935)

Military organizations, 14, 52, 55
Millay (Edna St. Vincent), (25)
Miller (Abbie C.), 40
Miller (William Rickarby), 22
Molitor (Joseph W.), 61
Monuments. See Buildings
Moore (Harry P.), 68
Mora (José M.), 11
Moss (John C.), 75
Mott (Hopper Striker), 20
Mount (William Sidney), 22
Mulberry Bend, 32
Murdock Collection of Steamboat Photographs, 44 (25)
Murdock (George Washington), 44
Muybridge (Eadweard), 65

N

Nadelman (Elie) Folk Art Collection, 22
Nagle (John T.), 32
Nankivell (Edith), 7
Nash (George W.), 20 (17)
Nast (Thomas), 10, 49
Native Americans, 11, 14, 27, 49, 68, 72 (29)
Naval History Society Collection, 68
Naval prints, 33, 47, 68
Negative File, 45 (22)
Negatives. See Photographs
Nesbitt (George F.), 22
New Jersey, 8, 21, 43, 53
New York City (NY), 1-5, 7-11, 13, 15-24, 26, 28, 31, 32, 34-37, 40, 42-45, 47-50, 53, 54-59, 61-66, 69-71, 73, 74
   Bronx, 5, 20, 43, 62, 63, 66, 69, 70
   Brooklyn, 20, 23, 24, 43, 69, 71
   Manhattan, 1, 2, 5, 7-9, 13, 15, 18, 20, 23, 24, 26, 28, 32, 34-37, 43, 48, 49, 56, 59, 62-66, 69, 70, 73, 74
   Queens, 20, 43, 63, 69
   Staten Island, 8, 20, 24, 43
New York City Board of Rapid Transit, 69 (19)
New York City Hall, 40, 69 (162)
New York Gallery of the Fine Arts, 22
New York Herald Tribune, 41

New-York Historical Society, 46 (16-19)
New-York Historical Society Pictorial Archive, 46 (18)
New York Life Insurance Building (26)
New York (State), 20, 21, 54, 58, 65
New York World's Fair, 1939-1940, 1, 45
News photographs, 34
Newsam (Albert), 25
Newsboys, 8 (13)
Niagara Falls, 20, 45
Night views, 9

O

Ogden (Beecher), 20
Ogden (Harry A.), 67, 68
Olds Collection of Naval Prints, 47 (19, 28)
Olds (Irving S.), 47
Opalotypes. See Photographs
Opper (Frederick B.), 29
Orchard Beach (NYC), 66
Osmanson (G.L.), 70

P

Pach Brothers, 20, 52 (19)
Palladiotypes. See Photographs
Pan-American Exposition, 2
Panoramic maps, 20
Paper roses. See Ephemera
Paper weights. See Ephemera
Parades and celebrations 1, 2, 8, 20, 32, 37, 45
Parish (Betty W.), 7
Parish (Daniel, Jr.), 40
Parkchester (NYC), 43
Parks, 20, 65 (171)
Parrish (Maxfield), 75
Patent medicines, 31
Patriotic envelopes. See Ephemera
Peabody & Stearns, 3
Penfield (Edward), 55
Pennell (Joseph), 35, 68 (172)
Penney (James), 7
Pennsylvania Station (NYC), 34, 48

NOTE: Index numbers refer to the entry numbers for the Collections, except for numbers in parentheses, which refer to pages in the introduction and indexes. Collection entry names are bold-faced

Figure 125. Etcher Joseph Pennell. Photograph by Pirie MacDonald, ca 1922. (MacDonald Collection, neg. no. 44851)

Pennsylvania Station Demolition Photograph Collection, 48 (25)
People. See Portraits, Street scenes
Peters Collection of Pictorial Newspaper Illustrations, 49 (13, 18, 28)
Peters (Harry T.), 49
Philippines, 41
Photographer File, 50 (23)
Photographers. See Albok (John); Alland (Alexander); Anson (Rufus); Anthony (E. & H.T.); Appleton (D. & Co.); Armbruster (Eugene L.); Bagoe (George T.); Beals (Jessie Tarbox); Bierstadt (Edward); Bogardus (Abraham); Bracklow (Robert L.); Brady (Mathew B.); Browning (Irving); Browning (Sam); Burger (Chester); Burton (Thomas J.); Canoune (Howard M.); Carbutt (John); Chapman (Arthur D.); Child (Edmund B.); Coleman (Daniel); Cotterell (Harry, Jr.); Cunningham (Bill); Dodd (George C.); Drucker & Baltes Co.; Dutcher (H.F.); Feininger (Andreas); Fredericks (Charles D.); Gambee (Robert); Gardner (Alexander); Genthe (Arnold); Gerdau (Carl); Gurney (Jeremiah); Hassler (William D.); Hatos (Alexander); Haynes (F. Jay); Hervey (Anotoinette B.); Hewitt (Mattie E.); Hine (Charles G.); Holmes (Silas); Huberland (Morris); Ingalls (Frank M.);

Jackson (William H.); Johnston (John S.);
Keep (Austin Baxter); Keystone View Co.;
Kilburn Brothers; Kilmer (Theron W.);
Langenheim Brothers; Langill Photo Co.;
Lawrence (Richard H.); Lester (Robert M.);
Levick Studio; Liberman (Herman N.);
Loonan (Alfred C.); MacDonald (Pirie);
Mackey (Chris); McIntosh (Burr);
McLaughlin Air Service; Molitor (Joseph W.);
Moore (Harry P.); Muybridge (Eadweard);
Nagle (John T.); Nash (George W.); Ogden
(Beecher); Osmanson (G.L.); Pach Brothers;
Piffard (Henry G.); Plumbe (John); Prevost
(Victor); Riis (Jacob); Rockwood (George
G.); Roege (William J.); Russell (Andrew J.);
Sarony (Napoleon); Scott (Ernest L.); Smith
(James Reuel); Smith (Richard A.); Smyth
(Frederick H.); Soule (John P.); Stonebridge
(George E.); Thomas Air Views; Thompson
(Frederick F.); Tiemann (Herman N.);
Trappan (John J.); Ulmann (Doris);
Underwood & Underwood; Vrooman (John
J.); Watkins (Carleton E.); Wenzel (Edward)
Photographs, 1-5, 8, 9, 11, 13, 15, 17-21, 23,
24, 26, 28-30, 32, 34, 36-39, 41-46, 50, 52,
54, 56, 59-63, 65-75 *(23-25)*
    albumen, 2, 11, 38, 65
    ambrotypes, 12
    cabinet cards, 2, 68
    calotypes, 56
    cartes de visite, 2, 11
    color, 36, 50, 61, 65, 70
    cyanotypes, 71
    daguerreotypes, 12
    Kodak prints, 2
    logbooks, 8, 24, 66, 71
    negatives, 1, 5, 8, 13, 19, 23, 24, 26, 28, 34, 36, 41-43, 45, 46, 48, 56, 60, 62, 63, 66, 71, 73, 74
    opalotypes, 12
    palladiotypes, 13
    panoramic, 45
    photomontage, 9
    platinum prints, 8, 13, 72
    prints, 1-4, 8, 9, 11, 13, 15, 17-21, 23, 24, 26, 28-30, 32, 36-39, 42-44, 46, 48, 50, 52, 54, 59-63, 65-69, 71-74
    stereographs, 2, 12, 28, 65, 70
    tintypes, 12, 65
    transparencies, 19, 65, 66, 70
    See also: Aerial photographs, Amateur photographers, Architectural photographs, Camera clubs, Fashion photographs, Landscape photographs, News photographs, Pictorial photographs, Still life photographs
Photogravures. *See* Prints
Photomechanical prints. *See* Prints
Photomontage. *See* Photographs
Pictorial lettersheets. *See* Ephemera
Pictorial newspapers, 49
Pictorial photographs, 13, 19, 72
Piffard (Henry G.), 32
Pintard, John, (16)
Piranesi (Giambattista), 40
Platinum prints. *See* Photographs
Playbills. *See* Ephemera
Playing cards. *See* Ephemera
Plumbe (John), 12
Politics, 10, 49, 55, 68
Polk (James K.), 25
Pollard Architectural Drawing Collection, 51 *(26)*
Pollard (Calvin), 51
Pool (Eugene H.), 68
Portrait File, 52 *(22, 162)*
Portraits, 2, 4, 6, 11, 12, 19, 25, 29, 30, 39, 41, 45, 47, 49, 52, 54, 57, 65, 67, 72
Post Architectural Record Collection, 53 *(12, 19, 26)*
Post (George B.), 53, 73
Post (William S.), 53
Postcard File, 54 *(28)*
Postcards, 4, 54
Poster File, 55 *(28)*
Posters, 31, 46, 55, 67
Potter (Henry C.), 13
Presidents, 10, 25, 52
Prevost (B.L.), 57
Prevost Photograph Collection, 56 *(18, 23)*
Prevost (Victor), 56
Printing Plate File, 57 *(28)*
Printing plates, 6, 57
Printmaker File, 58 *(27, 30)*
Printmakers. *See* Anderson (Alexander); Bachmann (John); Baillie (James); Bennett (William J.); Bien (Julius); Borne (Mortimer); Briem (Gottlob L.); Britton & Rey; Browne (Syd); Bufford (John H.); Burgis (William); Butler (George H.); Clay (Edward W.); Currier (Nathaniel); Currier & Ives; D'Avignon (Francis); Dawkins (Henry); Dehmann (Karl); Endicott & Co.; French (Edwin D.); Golinkin (Joseph); Hassam (Childe); Havell (Robert, Jr.); Hill (John); Himely (Sigismond); Hoff (Henry); Hunter (F. Leo); Imbert (Anthony); Karoly (Andrew); Kelloggs; Keppler (Joseph and Joseph Jr.); Kurz & Allison; Lankes (Julius J.); Longacre (James B.); Lowell (Nat); Macdonald (Arthur N.); Magnus (Charles); Maverick family; McNulty (William C.); Mielatz (Charles F.W.); Moss (John C.); Nankivell (Edith); Nesbitt (George F.); Newsam (Albert); Parish (Betty W.); Pennell (Joseph); Penney (James); Prevost (B.L.); Reich (Jacques); Revere (Paul); Robinson (Henry R.); Rosenthal (Albert); Rosenthal (Max); Roth (Ernest D.); Sachse (Edward); Sarony & Major; Sartain (John); Schutz (Anton); Simon (Thomas F.); Simonsen (Paul); Smillie (James D.); Smith (Sidney L.); Spenceley (J. Winfred); Stansbury (Arthur J.); Strickland (William); Strobridge Lithographing Company; Strong (Thomas W.); Wallace (William H.); Wetherill (Elisha K.K.); White (Charles H.); Whitefield (Edwin); Wittemann Albertype Co.; Wright (Charles Lennox)
Prints, 2, 6, 7, 10, 14, 20, 22, 25, 27, 29, 31, 33, 35, 38, 40, 46, 47, 49, 52, 54, 55, 58, 67, 68 75 *(27, 28)*
    aquatints, 47, 58
    chromolithographs, 29, 55, 67
    drypoints, 7
    engravings, 6, 10, 14, 22, 25, 27, 33, 40, 47, 58
    etchings, 7, 25, 35, 47, 58
    linoleum prints, 7
    lithographs, 7, 10, 14, 22, 25, 27, 33, 35, 38, 47, 54, 55, 58
    mezzotints, 47
    photogravures, 13, 25, 72
    photomechanical prints, 14, 19, 49, 54, 55, 65, 75
    wood engravings, 17, 49
    woodcuts, 7, 25, 27, 47, 49, 55, 58
    See also Naval prints
Public buildings. *See* Buildings
Public Service Commission, 69
Puck, 29
Pyle (Howard), 49, 75

Q

Queens (NYC). *See* New York City
Quinn (W. Johnson) Collection, 20

R

Railroads. *See* Transportation
Raymond (Henry Jarvis), 11
Recruiting posters, 55
Reeves (William F.), 20
Reich (Jacques), 52
Religious buildings. *See* Buildings
Remington (Frederic), 49
Renwick (James, Jr.), 3
Residential buildings. *See* Buildings
Revere (Paul), 58
Revolutionary War, 10, 46, 47, 68, 74
Rewards of merit. *See* Ephemera
Richardson (William S.), 42
Riis (Jacob), 32, 59
Riis Reference Photograph Collection, 59, (25, 163)
Robinson (Henry R.), 10
Rockwood (George G.), 11
Roege (William J.), 20, 24, 45
Rogers (John) family, 12, 52 (162)
Roosevelt (Theodore), 10
Rosborg (Christian F.), 3
Rosecliff (Newport, R.I.), 42
Rosenthal (Albert), 25, 52
Rosenthal (Max), 52
Roth (Ernest D.), 7 (18)
Russell (Andrew J.), 65
Russell (Lillian), 52

S

Sachse (Edward), 68
Saint-Mémin (Charles Balthazar Julien Févret de), 57
Salmagundi Club, 52
San Francisco (CA), 20
Sargeant (Edward A.), 53
Sarony & Major, 20
Sarony (Napoleon), 11, 52
Sartain (John), 25
Sauer (E.H.), 51
Savage (Edward), 47
Scandlin (W.I.), 56
Scanlon Collection of Steamboat Photographs, 60 (25)
Scanlon (Joseph), 60
Schermerhorn & Foulks, 3
Schermerhorn family, 12
Schutz (Anton), 7, 35
Schuyler family, 12
Scott (Ernest L.), 20, (14)
Seton (Harold), 52 (18)
Seventh Regiment (NY National Guard), 52
Shaw (Joshua), 58
Sheean (Oliver C.), 6
Sheet music covers. *See* Ephemera
Ships. *See* Transportation
Silhouettes, 52
Silver & Company Collection of Store Display Photographs, 61 (25)
Silver (Bertram S.), 61
Silver (S.S. & Co.), 61
Simon (Thomas F.), 35
Simonsen (Paul), 7
Singer Building (NYC), 28
Skyscrapers. *See* Buildings
Slavery, 68
Slums, 32, 59
Smillie (James D.), 58
Smith (James Kellum, Mrs.), 42
Smith (James Reuel), 62
Smith (Richard A.), 26 (25)
Smith (Sidney L.), 6
Smith Springs and Wells Photograph Collection, 62 (25, 163)
Smyth Collection of Fire Photographs, 63 (25)
Smyth (Frederick H.), 63
Snook Architectural Record Collection, 64 (19, 26)
Snook (John B.), 64
Snook (Thomas E.), 64
Society of Amateur Photographers of NY, 8, 32
Society of Iconophiles, 58

NOTE: Index numbers refer to the entry numbers for the Collections, except for numbers in parentheses, which refer to pages in the introduction and indexes. Collection entry names are bold-faced.

SoHo (NYC), 73
Soule (John P.), 65
South Street, (30)
Souvenir viewbooks, 20
Spanish-American War, 8, 41, 65, 68
Speakeasy cards. *See* Ephemera
Spenceley (J. Winfred), 6
Sports, 17, 32, 49, 65, 68
Springs, 62
Stansbury (Arthur J.), 58
Staten Island (NYC). *See* New York City
Statue of Liberty (NYC), 31 (22)
Steamboats. *See* Transportation
Stereograph File, 65 (23, 34, 164)
Stereographs. *See* Photographs
Stewart (Alexander T.), 64
Still life photographs, , 72
Stock Exchange, 24, 35

Figure 126. Mr. Stonebridge and his dog in front of Zbrowski Mansion, Claremont Park, N.Y.. Glass negative ca. 1903. (Stonebridge Collection, neg. no. 63861-1763)

Stonebridge (George E.), 66, 70 (174)
Stonebridge (George E., Mrs.), 66
Stonebridge Photograph Collection, 66 (19, 25, 174)
Stores. *See* Buildings, commercial
Street scenes, 1, 2, 4, 5, 7-9, 15, 18, 20, 23, 24, 28, 31, 32, 34-37, 45, 49, 50, 54, 56, 58, 59, 62, 63, 65, 66, 69, 70, 73, 74
Strickland (William), 3
Strikes, 34
Strobridge (James G.), 67
Strobridge Lithographing Company, 67
Strobridge Lithographing Company Poster Collection, 67 (12, 36)

Strong (Thomas W.), 10
Subject File, 68 *(22, 27, 170)*
Subway Construction Photograph Collection, 69 *(25)*
Subways. *See* Transportation
Supreme Court Justices, 25

T

Tammany Hall, 29
Theater, 9, 11, 17, 29, 31, 41, 51, 52, 55, 67
Thomas Air Views *(31)*
Thompson (Frederick F.), 65 *(34)*
Thumb (Tom), 2
Thulstrup (Thure de), 49
Thursby (Emma) family, 12, 52
Tiemann (Herman N.), 20, 45
Times Square (NYC), 5, 9, 34, 50 *(6)*
Tintypes. *See* Photographs
Tobacco, 31
Tobacco tins. *See* Ephemera
Trade cards. *See* Ephemera
Trade catalogs. *See* Ephemera
Transparencies. *See* Photographs
Transparency File, 70 *(23)*
Transportation, 2, 3, 5, 9, 18, 20, 23, 24, 31, 43-45, 47-49, 51, 54, 60, 65, 68, 69
    buses, 18 *(169)*
    elevated railroads, 3, 5, 20, 22, 23
    ferries, 44, 60
    railroads, 48, 65
    ships and steamboats, 24, 33, 44, 47, 54, 60, 68 *(170)*
    subways, 20, 69
Trappan (John J.), 71
Trappan Photograph Collection, 71 *(25)*
Trappan (Ruth), 8, 71
Trench (Joseph), 64
Trumbull (John), 3
Truth (Sojourner), 11
Tutchings (Everett, Mr. and Mrs.), 39

U

Ulmann (Doris), 72
Ulmann Foundation, 72
Ulmann Photograph Collection, 72 *(12, 19, 23)*
Underwood & Underwood, 65
Union Square (NYC), 37
United States, 20, 49, 54, 65, 68

United States Bicentennial, 17
United States Capitol (Washington, D.C.), 3
United States Coast Guard, 38
Upjohn (Richard), 3
Upper West Side (NYC), 8

V

Van Altena (Edward), 70
Vanderbilt Ball, 52
Vanitie Beauty Shop, *(32)*
Vaux (Calvert), 3
Vice presidents, 25
Views, 1, 2, 4, 5, 7-9, 11, 19, 20, 24, 33, 43, 45, 47, 49, 54, 57, 58, 65, 70, 73 *See also* Street scenes
Visscher (Cornelis), 27
Vitarius (Ilona Albok), 1
Von Kienbusch (C. Otto), *(19)*
Vrooman (John J.), 20
Vues d'optique, 20

W

Wall Street (NYC), 35, 36
Wall (William G.), 58
Wallace (William H.), 7
War of 1812, 47, 68
Warren & Wetmore, 3
Wars, 2, 47, 55, 65, 68
Washington Heights (NYC), 2
Watchpapers. *See* Ephemera
Waterfronts. *See* Harbors
Watkins (Carleton E.), 65
Weed (Gertrude and Raphael), 52 *(18)*
Weindorf (Arthur), 20
Weisman Collection of Architectural Photographs, 73 *(25)*
Weisman (Winston R.), 73
Wells, 62
Wenzel (Edward), 74
Wenzel Photograph Collection, 74 *(25)*
West Point (NY), 2, 20
Western states, 2, 65, 68
Westervelt (Leonidas), 52
Wetherill (Elisha K.K.), 7
White (Charles H.), 7
White (Lawrence Grant), 42
White (Stanford), 42
Whitefield (Edwin), 20
Whitman (Walt), 52

Figure 127. Rose and Duane Streets, New York City. Photograph by unidentified photographer, ca. 1890. (Geographic File, neg. no. 50709)

Wittemann Albertype Co., 54
Women, 41, 49, 52, 68
Wood engravings. *See* Prints
Woodcuts. *See* Prints
Woolworth Building (NYC), 21
World War I, 55, 68
World War II, 1, 55, 68
World's Fairs. *See* Crystal Palace, New York World's Fair, Pan-American Exposition
World Trade Center (NYC), 36
Worth (Thomas), 57
Wright (Charles Lennox), 75
Wright (Charles Lennox II), 75
Wright Photomechanical Printing Collection, 75 *(28)*
Wyoming, 65

Y

Yewell (George Henry), 22
York and Sawyer, 46
Young (Art), 29

Z

Zabriskie (George A.), 2